GROWING TOWARD
SPIRITUAL MATURITY

**Other Evangelical Training Association
books from Crossway Books**

Exploring the Old Testament
Exploring the New Testament
Exploring Church History
Exploring the Basics of the Bible
Evidence and Truth
Biblical Truth
The One True God: Father, Son, and Holy Spirit
Biblical Ethics: Choosing Right in a World Gone Wrong

BIBLICAL ESSENTIALS

GROWING TOWARD SPIRITUAL MATURITY

GARY C. NEWTON

CROSSWAY BOOKS

A DIVISION OF
GOOD NEWS PUBLISHERS
WHEATON, ILLINOIS

Growing Toward Spiritual Maturity

Copyright © 2004 by Evangelical Training Association

Published by Crossway Books
    a division of Good News Publishers
    1300 Crescent Street
    Wheaton, Illinois 60187

Previously published by Evangelical Training Association, copyright © 1999.

Cover design: Josh Dennis

Cover photo: Ric Ergenbright

First printing 2004

Printed in the United States of America

Library of Congress Cataloging-in-Publication Data
Newton, Gary C., 1951–
    Growing toward spiritual maturity / Gary C. Newton.
      p. cm.
    Previously published: Wheaton, Ill. : Evangelical Training Association,
©1999. Originally published ©1988 under title.
    Includes bibliographical references.
    ISBN 1-58134-571-2 (alk. paper)
    1. Witness bearing (Christianity) 2. Sanctification. I. Title.
BV4520.G76   2004
248.4—dc22   2003022699

CH		13	12	11	10	09	08	07	06	05	04
15	14	13	12	11	10	9	8	7	6	5	4	3	2	1

CONTENTS

Foreword

RICHARD FOSTER'S CLASSIC work *Celebration of Discipline* includes a word from the author humbly confessing the weakness of words on paper as we struggle to grasp the miracle of grace as God transforms lives. The most eloquent of scholars among us cannot completely do justice to the message of God's Word. You are strongly urged to read and study the lessons within this brief text with an open Bible at hand. Numerous Scripture references will be cited, and some will be quoted. Perhaps the Holy Spirit will call to your mind many other passages to reinforce the growth principles presented herein.

Secondly, you will note the publisher has chosen to keep the term *church* lowercase in all instances. This does not represent any diminished enthusiasm for honoring Christ's work nor His Bride. Generally, capitalization may be used to refer to the universal body of believers. This book extensively notes principles related to all believers *and* to local assemblies. In some cases, Scripture means for both to overlap. We refer you to Ryken, Wilhoit, and Longman's definition (*Dictionary of Biblical Imagery*, IVP): "The church is the partial fulfillment of the kingdom of God in the here and now and serves as a primary agent of the kingdom; hence it is appropriate to apply some kingdom imagery to the church itself (e.g., Col. 1:13)." For that reason, the jockeying of capitalization has been overruled to avoid confusion.

Finally, this text and its accompanying study materials are designed to integrate the inward disciplines with our outward expressions of spiritual maturity. The author rightly cautions Christians against unbalanced attention to the fruit of the Spirit observable by others. This text is appropriately named:

Growing—because maturity is a lifelong process;

Toward—because our vision must be fixed on Christ;

Spiritual—because inward transformation determines our growth;

Maturity—because fulfillment of the Great Commission is our task.

May you find the joy of the Lord in your journey.

Yvonne E. Thigpen

I.

FOUNDATIONS FOR
SPIRITUAL GROWTH

1

The Dynamics of Spiritual Growth

A STRATEGY FOR growing toward Christlikeness must be based on the actual ways that people grow and develop spiritually. By identifying and understanding how we spiritually mature, we become more intentional in our use of time and methods. Understanding the dynamics of spiritual growth makes us more aware of how God uses the specific circumstances of our lives to draw us closer to Himself.

In this first chapter we will identify eight principles of spiritual growth. Each principle helps us unravel God's mystery of transforming sinful, rebellious people into godly, passionate lovers of His Son, Jesus. Each of these principles is grounded both in Scripture and in common experience.

1. *God is ultimately responsible for all spiritual growth.*

There is a dangerous tendency within this sophisticated, technological culture to attribute spiritual "success stories" to clever human strategies, wise choices, or determined hard work. Without downplaying the importance of human responsibility in spiritual growth, God's role must always be central.

This principle shines forth clearly in Isaiah 61:11, where the prophet Isaiah compares God's role in dealing with His people to the role of garden soil in causing seeds to grow. God plays the role of a seasoned farmer, carefully preparing the soil and maintaining the garden with the vision to see each seed grow into maturity.

This principle is also clearly illustrated in the New Testament. When Paul saw the early church members focusing too much on the role of human leaders, he reminded them that God is the person primarily responsible for growth. The picture in 1 Corinthians 3:7-9 is also of a garden. There are many servants helping the Gardener (God) grow His seeds; yet it is the Gardener who causes the growth. The Christian's attitude toward growth should always give tribute for the growth to God. Paul teaches, in 1 Corinthians 15:10, that everything the Christian becomes or accomplishes for the kingdom of God is only because of God's grace and power.

We are saved by grace because of what God did rather than anything we could contribute. Yet it seems to be difficult for Christians to believe that their continued spiritual growth is dependent on God. A subtle legalism often creeps into our lives that equates our spiritual growth with the disciplines we exercise. Paul challenges the Christians of his time with a message relevant for us today: "Are you so foolish? After beginning with the Spirit, are you now trying to attain your goal by human effort?" (Gal. 3:3).

God is ultimately responsible for the growth process in our lives from beginning to end. He chose before the world was created to make us a part of His garden where we could grow into the holy likeness of His Son, Jesus (Eph. 1:4). His plan was not only to save us, as important as that transformational experience is, but also to continue to nurture us into His likeness. His role as the Gardener is not finished when the seed takes root. Rather, His role in our spiritual development has just begun.

The Holy Spirit works as a supernatural catalyst throughout our life. He first brings us into a personal relationship with Jesus and then molds us into His likeness. "He who began a good work in you will carry it on to completion until the day of Christ Jesus" (Phil. 1:6). God is ultimately responsible for all spiritual growth in the believer's life.

2. *Effort, diligence, and discipline are absolutely necessary for growth.*

If God is responsible for our growth, can we simply bask in the glory of His grace, waiting for Him to propel us into His orbit of holiness and bliss? Paradoxically, God's complete provision for our growth is not undercut by the necessity of our effort and discipline. In fact, Scripture seems to suggest that our diligence is essential to the growth process.

In 2 Peter 1:1-11, we learn that God is both the source and dynamo for godly living. Additionally we are challenged to "make every effort" to build on what God has given. God's provision for our growth becomes the *reason* why we should diligently work toward Christlike qualities. While God supplies the resources and enablement for our growth, we must supply the effort.

Paul also emphasizes this principle in both his personal lifestyle and teachings. He often uses the example of a soldier or athlete to illustrate the amount of discipline and hard work required to be successful. In 1 Corinthians 9:24-27, Paul states that "in a race all the runners run, but only one gets the prize." He then goes on to challenge his readers to run the Christian race in such a way as to get the prize. This demands strict training, much like the focus of today's Olympic games. Concluding with an example from his own life, Paul says that he "beats" (meaning "to conquer;" see Rom. 8:13) his body to keep it submissive to God's will for his life. His training plan is not sporadic, like a man beating the air, but it is intentional and deliberate. In order to grow into a mature woman or man of God, the believer must be in a diligent training plan for growth (1 Tim. 4:7-8). We can learn a great deal about growing toward Christian maturity from both the example and teaching of a godly man like Paul.

This close relationship between God's provision for our growth and our active involvement in the process is nowhere more clear than in Philippians 2:12-13: "Continue to work out your salvation with fear and trembling, for it is God who works in you to will and to act according to his good purpose." The mystery of this principle may be hard to grasp, but the implication is clear. If Christians are to grow toward maturity in Christ, they must demonstrate their passion to grow by obedient action.

3. *Spiritual growth potential may not be easy to see at first.*

Anyone who has ever worked with junior high students knows that it is dangerous to predetermine who will become the Christian leaders of the future. I have seen some of the most athletic, popular, and brilliant students fail miserably in their Christian walk, and I have also seen some of the most unlikely students blossom into Christian giants. God's standards for success are different from ours.

As we evaluate our lives, we must be careful not to underestimate what God can do in and through us. Rather than compare ourselves to spiritual giants at the end of their pilgrimages, we would be wiser to acknowledge where those people began their walk with God. When Samuel was looking for God's choice to replace Saul as king of Israel, he was tempted to choose David's older brother Eliab. However, God clearly rebuked Samuel for his lack of spiritual discernment. "Do not consider his appearance or his height, for I have rejected him. The LORD does not look at the things man looks at. Man looks at the outward appearance, but the LORD looks at the heart" (1 Sam. 16:7). Who could have guessed that a red-haired shepherd boy would become the most famous king in the history of Israel?

Paul, in his first letter to the Corinthian church, responds to their preoccupation with the more external qualities for leadership (1 Cor. 1:26-29). God does not confine His assignments only to the brightest and the best. Rather, He chooses people who have a heart to follow Him regardless of their natural abilities or talents.

There is a dangerous practice in contemporary ministries to focus discipleship efforts only on those who have the highest potential. While the intent may be to avoid wasting time on followers *we* perceive to be insincere, there is a danger of discouraging someone God could powerfully use. In His parable of the weeds, Jesus tells the story of a man who sowed good seed in a field. While he was sleeping, an enemy planted bad seed in with the good seed. When the different seeds began to sprout, both good and bad plants sprang up. The farmer's servants asked him if they should get rid of the bad plants, and he responded: "No, because while you are pulling the weeds, you may root up the wheat with them. Let both grow together until the harvest. At that time I will tell the harvesters: First collect the weeds and tie them in bundles to be burned; then gather the wheat and bring it into my barn" (Matt. 13:29-30). In the early stage of a believer's growth, it may be difficult to see evidence of the Holy Spirit at work. In fact, it may be difficult to see a lot of difference between a new Christian and someone living for the world. Time will bring out the true quality of the heart.

Jesus emphasizes this principle again in His next parable about the mustard seed (Matt. 13:31-32). God enjoys making something great out of something small. Who would ever imagine that a tiny mustard seed would produce a gigantic tree? From a human perspective, the small things in this world are rarely important. In God's eyes, however, they can develop into great harvests. We must never underestimate what God can do in our lives or in the lives of others because He sees tremendous growth potential in every believer who has a heart for Him.

4. *Spiritual growth depends on an intimate relationship with Jesus Christ.*

Evangelical Christianity has always taught that a relationship with Christ is absolutely necessary for salvation. The relationship must continue beyond this initial introduction. Salvation is only the first step in a long journey of intimacy with our Lord. As important as a marriage ceremony is to the marriage relationship, intimacy in marriage goes much deeper than either the vows or the honeymoon. Growth in the Christian life requires an ongoing intimacy in one's relationship with Christ.

Jesus gives us a clear illustration of the link between growth and a close relationship with Him in John 15:1-17. Here Jesus describes Himself as the vine and Christians as the branches. The principle repeated over and over again in this passage is that the only way to grow and bear fruit in our lives is to stay closely attached to the vine. The term for staying closely attached is translated among versions as "remain," "abide," "continue," or "dwell." These terms clearly describe the responsibility of the Christian to stay closely connected to Jesus throughout life—as an ongoing relationship of intimate communion and fellowship.

In this passage Jesus describes at least five benefits of staying closely connected. The first benefit is fruitfulness in our lives (vv. 2, 3, 4, 5, 8, 18). From Galatians 5:22-23, we discover that fruitfulness is at least in part associated with the fruit of the Spirit. These are exhibited primarily through our character and its outflow into the lives of others. Evidence of this fruit is directly related to our goal of maturity in Christ. As a Christian matures, increasingly more fruit should be exhibited.

The second benefit is found in verse 4: "Remain in me, and I will remain in you." As we stay close to the Lord, He promises to stay close to us. What a promise! In a day when relationships are becoming less and less secure, Christ gives us a way to enjoy absolute security.

The third benefit of maintaining an intimate relationship with Jesus is answered prayer. "If you remain in me and my words remain in you, ask whatever you wish, and it will be given you" (v. 7). The best way to explain this benefit is to recall your relationship with a close friend. The closer two people are to each other, the more sensitive they tend to be to each other's needs. As we get closer to the Lord, the more our thoughts and desires become like His, and the more His will is accomplished through us and our prayers.

The fourth benefit of walking in a close and intimate relationship is what Jesus terms "joy" (v. 11). More than simple happiness, based on circumstances, the joy that Jesus describes relates to a supernatural inner peace that brings emotional satisfaction even in the midst of the most distressing circumstances. This joy reflects a deep satisfaction based on a person's assurance of the presence of God in one's life.

The fifth benefit of staying close to Jesus and obeying His Word is friendship with Jesus. As He says, "You are my friends if you do what I command. I no longer call you servants, because a servant does not know his master's business. Instead, I have called you friends, for everything that I learned from my Father I have made known to you" (vv. 14-15). At this level of friendship with Jesus, He enables His disciples to discern God's Word with more clarity and insight. The former sting of legalism and false guilt is replaced with a sense of freedom and partnership. Friends of Jesus enjoy all the rich blessings of intimacy with the King of Kings and Lord of Lords.

5. *Growth is primarily an inside-out process.*

Growth relates more to the condition of a person's heart on the inside than to what a person encounters from the outside. Biblical content, experience, and relationships help us grow only as we interact and respond from the heart under the illumination of the Holy Spirit. Principles of growth are learned only as we wrestle to integrate them into the core of our being. Since the beginning of recorded biblical history, God has challenged humankind to offer wholehearted worship and service (Deut. 6:4-6). Loving, serving, and worshiping God are actions that arise from a heart of passion. Our challenge is to kindle the spiritual fire within our hearts.

Once again we turn to Jesus' parables for insight. In His story of the sower (or, more appropriately, the Parable of the Soils), Jesus explains the dynamics of spiritual growth using the familiar garden analogy (Mark 4:1-20). Although common interpretation of this text focuses on the role of the sower, Jesus identifies the soil as the most significant factor in spiritual formation. Four different types of soil are represented in the text: (1) hard soil on the path, (2) rocky, shallow soil, (3) weedy soil, (4) good soil. The different soils represent the different conditions of human hearts related to their receptivity to the gospel message (or the "seed"). Jesus' main purpose in telling this parable to the disciples is to explain the dynamics of how and why spiritual growth occurs differently among people. How growth occurs, or whether or not it occurs at all, depends to a great degree on the condition of the heart. When one's heart is soft and receptive to spiritual things, the ability to understand and assimilate the Word is heightened. Spiritual growth begins in the heart and moves to outward expressions of growth.

6. *Spiritual growth relates to every aspect of our lives.*

What begins inside the person eventually affects every aspect of life—family, friendships, work, leisure, and business. God's desire is that all His children love Him with their whole being—body, mind, and spirit (Deut. 6:5). Spiritual growth, seen in this light, is a process in which people willingly allow the Holy Spirit to control increasingly more of their lives.

Spiritual growth also relates to all aspects of personal development. Once again Jesus provides us with a perfect example of this process as recorded in Luke 2:52: "And Jesus grew in wisdom and stature, and in favor with God and men." Although this simple description of Jesus' growth process is not meant to include every category of human development, it does suggest that growth is multidimensional. We can conclude that it involves the intellectual, physical, spiritual, and relational categories as named by today's social scientists. This principle of multidimensional growth is clearly seen throughout the Old and New Testaments. The continual cry of the prophets of the Old Testament is not only for Israel to return to God but also to show evidence of godliness in practical action (Zech. 7:9-10). Spiritual growth and maturity express themselves in both belief and action.

Throughout the New Testament we find this principle repeated in various contexts. John the Baptist challenges people not only to "repent" (Matt. 3:2), but also to "produce fruit in keeping with repentance" (Matt. 3:8). The challenge here is to change one's heart and belief system as well as one's behavior. Coming to God and growing in godliness demand our whole being. Jesus reiterates the multidimensional nature of commitment to God when addressing a Jewish lawyer in Matthew 22:34-40. Samuel Shoemaker states that "we begin the actual Christian experience when we surrender as much of ourselves as we can to as much of Christ as we understand."[1] A simple commitment grows into an ever broadening stream of fullness of the Holy Spirit that transforms us, by God's grace, into greater conformity to Christ's likeness.

Paul calls this transformation process the "renewing of your mind" (Rom. 12:1-2). He states that it begins with offering our bodies to Christ as "living sacrifices," refusing to follow the pagan lifestyle of the world. Regardless of how philosophers and theologians subdivide the nature of persons (body, mind, and/or soul), Scripture clearly teaches that growing in Christ involves every aspect of our personhood and life.

7. *Growth happens most naturally within a close social context.*

It is no surprise that close-knit families and churches are nurturing nests for strong, growing Christians. Characterized by love,

Christianity is learned primarily within the laboratory of human relationships. A family provides the most natural environment for children to learn to love and honor God. God's plan has always been for parents to model, teach, and train their children within the intimacy of the home. In Deuteronomy 6:6-9, Moses instructs the leaders of each family unit in ancient Israel to first model their faith in front of their children and then to teach or impress God's commandments on them, talking about them informally throughout daily activities, and finally to post reminders throughout the house of God's laws. The home combined both formal and informal teaching and was designed to be the richest educational environment for members to naturally learn to worship, love, and obey God.

An examination of both history and contemporary experience reveals that even Christian parents fail to live up to their biblical responsibilities. When children grow up in an atmosphere of emotional warmth and encouragement (with appropriate boundaries), they are more apt to respond to the teachings of Christ as modeled by their parents. When children do not have the privilege of growing up in such a home, a compelling need to find this warmth and love in other places will develop. Such needs often lead to unwholesome fulfillments.

God provides the context of the multigenerational family of God as our opportunity to learn, grow, and develop into Christlikeness. Healthy local churches provide a community where people of all ages, walks of life, ethnicity, and vocations learn together to love God and other persons. This principle of diversity is clearly demonstrated by the dynamics of the first church in Jerusalem. As you read Acts 2:42-47, observe the evidences of the quality of their community and its influence on the people in the surrounding areas.

One of the primary reasons for the growth of the early church was the sense of community its members enjoyed. People develop best when they belong to a close, caring, and committed group. People also learn best when they wrestle together with issues that are of immediate concern. The early church realized that the only way they could fulfill the Great Commission and infiltrate a pagan world was by being unified as the family of God. Fellowship and community were strategic factors in the growth of the early church. The term *fellowship* from the Greek word *koinonia* was used to express the common partnership between fellow believers because of their close relationship with Jesus Christ.

Paul explains the dynamics of the body of Christ in helping people to grow in Ephesians 4:11-16. As leaders in the church train people to serve and minister to one another, individuals in the fellowship are built up in unity and the knowledge of Christ. When members of the body of Christ lovingly interact with one another, they become more Christlike. Each person's common relationship with Jesus Christ and the use of gifts and abilities in a significant way are what hold the body of Christ together. Analyzing this passage from an educator's perspective helps us see that people learn and grow when they are trained by experienced, older mentors; they are involved in a close, caring group; they are encouraged by their peers; they interact with significant other people; they use what they are learning on a daily basis; and they see significance in what they are learning and doing in the lives of others.

8. *Significant growth occurs within the context of frustration, suffering, or challenge.*

One major contribution educational psychology has made to the field of Christian education is a more objective understanding of observations about how people learn. Simple reflection on the history of Christianity shows that persecution has made the church stronger. Some social science research has attempted to explain why this is so. Learning theorists point out that the only way some living organisms actually grow (or change) is by encountering an obstacle big enough to make them rethink the way they previously dealt with things. When faced with such challenges, the organism experiences initial frustration and discouragement. Yet through a process of trial and error and evaluating options, the organism will eventually either overcome the obstacle or be controlled by it. Based on the assumption that all living organisms learn in similar ways, it is easy to apply this principle to people.

There is ample evidence in Scripture also to point to the principle that we often grow most through difficult times. In 2 Thessalonians 1:3, Paul commends the faith of those in the church. In the next verse Paul tells us what was taking place in their community that precipitated their growth: "Therefore, among God's churches we boast about your perseverance and faith in all the persecutions and trials you are enduring." Throughout church history, persecution and suffering have only served to make the church stronger and more resilient.

Suffering is presented as a necessary and even normal part of the

Christian's life. Romans 8:18-27 gives a clear theological rationale for the reality of suffering. Paul continues developing our understanding in Philippians 1:29 by stating, "For it has been granted to you on behalf of Christ not only to believe on him, but also to suffer for him."

While it is definitely true that suffering may be a part of the *cost* of following Jesus, it may be helpful to discover some positive *reasons* for suffering. A significant clue comes from Hebrews 5:8-9. Here the author explains one of the purposes of suffering in Jesus' life. Christ, as both fully God and fully man, learned in the same way that we learn. He learned to obey His Father, the text says, through His suffering. After a life of perfect obedience, in the midst of severe suffering, He became the source of salvation for those who would follow in His footsteps. We cannot expect to learn any easier than did our Master.

Suffering, then, is to be seen as an opportunity to learn obedience. The tests of suffering give us the chance to strengthen our faith in the Word of God rather than trust our feelings. Suffering becomes an instrument of pruning in our growth process to help us change more directly into the likeness of Christ. If our goal is to become more Christlike and to know God more intimately, suffering is inevitable. Paul makes this connection very clear in Philippians 3:10-11: "I want to know Christ and the power of his resurrection and the fellowship of sharing in his sufferings, becoming like him in his death, and so, somehow, to attain to the resurrection from the dead." Intimacy with Christ is closely connected with both the experience of the power of the Holy Spirit and the experience of suffering.

Suffering can be appreciated as a valuable part of the gift of salvation only if we understand how it helps us learn, grow, and develop more into Christlikeness. God uses suffering and persecution in our lives to challenge us to higher levels of spiritual thinking and living. Seen in this light, suffering moves us closer to our goal of Christlikeness. Suffering and persecution challenge the reasons why we follow the Lord. It might be relatively easy to obey God's Word when it is profitable, it makes us feel good, or it brings us popularity, but the experience of suffering usually challenges these carnal motivations. Staying obedient to the Lord in the midst of suffering or temptation, Christians can strengthen their faith. "Blessed is the man who perseveres under trial, because when he has stood the test, he will receive the crown of life that God has promised to those who love him" (Jas. 1:12).

SUMMARY

In this chapter we have examined eight ways people grow and develop into maturity in Christ. These principles can be used to help us understand how God is working in our lives personally. This understanding will enable us to design more intentional learning strategies with those around us.

FOR FURTHER DISCUSSION

1. Which of the eight ways that people grow and develop is the most significant for you personally?
2. Identify a time in your life when you grew the most and explain why.
3. What do you think are the consequences when a person who claims to be a Christian refuses to put forth any effort to grow?
4. Why is it that many people don't really grow until they hit a difficult obstacle in life?
5. Identify the characteristics of a class experience or a group experience that had a significant influence on your life spiritually.

2

Becoming a Disciple of Jesus Christ

BEFORE WE BEGIN TO understand *how* to become something, we must have a clear picture of *what* it is that we want to become. This chapter describes first what a disciple is and then what it means to become a disciple of Jesus Christ.

WHAT IS A DISCIPLE?

The word *disciple* comes from the Greek word *mathetes*, meaning "learner, pupil, follower, or apprentice." This same Greek root is used for *math*, meaning "to learn." Thus, *mathematics* is understood to mean "thought accompanied by endeavor."[1] To become a disciple, therefore, means to follow someone and to learn from the person. An apprenticeship involves imitating one's master teacher. The process of how we learn or how we become like another person is at the very heart of the process of becoming a disciple.

Scripture uses the term *disciple* in different ways, depending on the context. At least eight different uses of the term are found throughout the Old and New Testaments:

1. *Followers of a leader*—Those who followed various leaders like Moses, John the Baptist, rabbis, Pharisees, and Jesus (John 1:35, 37).

2. *Various types of followers of Jesus*—The gospel writers describe general followers (Luke 6:13), serious believers (John 9:27), Joseph of Arimathea (Matt. 27:57), Ananias (Acts 9:10), Dorcas (Acts 9:36), and large groups of interested seekers (Luke 6:17).

3. *The apostles*—Often used in a formal sense to mean "the twelve," the specially chosen leaders that Jesus appointed to be closest to Him

and to lead the Great Commission after His death, resurrection, and ascension (Luke 6:13).

4. *Superficial, shallow, or simply curious followers*—People with a casual level of commitment to Jesus. When He says something they do not like, they leave Him. In this case, the usage may be similar to students in a modern classroom who are physically present in class but not serious about learning (John 6:60, 64, 66, 71).

5. *Known traitors with false motives*—Probably one of the most controversial personalities is Judas Iscariot. Interestingly, he is named as both a disciple and a member of "the twelve" (John 12:4).

6. *Sincere followers who made serious mistakes and failed often*—This is where we find Peter. Although he was committed from the heart to follow Jesus, he made many serious mistakes (Luke 22:31, 32, 57, 60-62).

7. *Jesus' exclusive use of the term "my disciple"*—From the beginning of His ministry, Jesus began to create, through modeling and teaching, a unique picture of what His disciples should be like. That distinctive picture is developed through stories, parables, illustrations, sermons, and question-and-answer sessions. The further He gets into His ministry, the more precisely He describes what it means to be *His* follower. At several times in His ministry, Jesus intentionally challenged large groups of curious followers to consider the cost of being a *true* follower. By analyzing what Jesus says are the characteristics of "my disciple," we gain a clearer picture of what He considered the major distinctives of His definition.

The first time Jesus is recorded using the term "my disciple" is in Luke 14:25-33. He had just finished telling the parable of the great banquet, indicating that the kingdom of God was going to include many who were not originally expecting to come. Multitudes were following Him who apparently were not serious about Jesus' mission. Jesus seems to be thinning out the crowds by teaching what it means to be "my disciple." In this passage, Jesus identifies three principles to follow to be His disciple. A person must:

1. Love Christ far above all other human relationships (v. 26).
2. Follow Christ even if it means suffering and death (v. 27).
3. Give everything to Christ (v. 33).

Jesus makes it clear that to follow Him, they must commit their whole self to Him. A disciple puts the relationship with Jesus Christ above every other relationship, follows Christ no matter what the cost, and gives everything (spiritual gifts and skills) for the kingdom of God.

Three other texts that record Jesus' use of "my disciple" describe evidences of a *true* disciple. The first of the three texts is John 8:31-32: "If you hold to my teaching, you are really my disciples. Then you will know the truth, and the truth will set you free." The phrase "hold to" is translated in other biblical versions as "abide" or "continue." Jesus challenged "the Jews who had believed him" to become His disciples by "holding to" or "continuing in" His teaching. Apparently Jesus saw a significant difference between those who merely listened to His teaching and those who lived by or obeyed His teaching. True disciples would continue to live by the principles Jesus taught. Obedience to Jesus' teaching is at the heart of being a disciple of Jesus.

The second text relating to evidence of being a disciple is found in John 13:34-35. True disciples model the same kind of love that Christ showed them. Love is the test of a true disciple.

Again in John 15:8, Jesus gives us a third test of a true disciple. The context is the illustration of the vine and the branches. Jesus says, "This is to my Father's glory, that you bear much fruit." This statement indicates that others will recognize true disciples by the fruit in those disciples' lives.

A follower of Jesus, then, loves Him above all other human relationships, is willing to suffer or even die for Him, and gives everything he or she owns to Christ. A true disciple of Jesus is recognized by steadfast obedience, love, and a fruitful life. While this standard of discipleship is obviously beyond any standard we can achieve on our own, Christ establishes it as our goal. Jesus' standard of discipleship must be the standard for the church today.

8. *The term* disciple *changes to* Christian—The term *disciple* was commonly used in the early church until the beginning of Paul's ministry. After the first persecution in the early church, the stoning of Stephen, the disciples scattered all over the Mediterranean world. As the church grew in the Greek city of Antioch, Barnabas was sent from Jerusalem to teach the new believers. He, in turn, called Paul to help him instruct the rapidly growing Gentile church there. It was in Antioch that the disciples were first called Christians (Acts 11:26).

We can only speculate as to the reasons for the change in terminology for Jesus' followers. Some scholars have suggested that the Gentile believers wanted a name that was not associated with the distinctive Jewish culture. Others suggest the terminology could have been changed to eliminate ambiguity associated with the more general term *disciple.* Perhaps the use of *Christian* may have been seen as more descriptive of who they were following. Within the Roman world, *-ian* added to the end of a proper name signified giving total allegiance to that person. Thus *Christian* became a very clear term connecting absolute loyalty with Christ. Used in this way, *Christian* seems more clear than *disciple.*

Whatever the reasons for the change, *disciple* was not used again in the New Testament after the book of Acts. Throughout the early church period until the time of the Roman emperor Constantine, the word *Christian* carried the same distinctive meaning that was associated with Jesus' use of "my disciple." Many Christians died for their faith at the hand of Roman authorities. To be a Christian meant a willingness to give everything for Jesus, even life itself. Persecution and suffering only served to make Christians stronger.

After Constantine declared Christianity to be the official religion of the Roman Empire, the term *Christian* began to lose its distinctive biblical meaning. Christianity grew more politically correct and lost its radical edge. From that time until now, the number of people who call themselves Christians has increased dramatically, but the standard for a true Christian has lowered drastically. A solution for some theologians today has been to use the term *Christian* to describe the "entry level" believer and to use the term *disciple* only for the "serious Christian." Unfortunately, this only leads to more confusion. The terms *Christian* and *disciple* must never lose their original meanings. The accurate picture of a disciple of Jesus must be clearly ingrained in our minds.

BECOMING A DISCIPLE OF JESUS

Another key to understanding how we grow into mature disciples of Jesus Christ is to realize that it is a process. The initial process begins with an integration of all eight of the spiritual growth principles discussed in the last chapter. Although the early stages of growth may be hard to see, God produces great things from small beginnings. The key to continued growth as a disciple of Jesus is in the quality of our relationship with Him. That relationship is defined by the attitude of our heart rather than external rituals and duties. Growth begins inside and spreads to encompass our whole life. Relationships with other like-minded followers of Jesus serve as catalysts to this growth. God may even use discouragement, persecution, or suffering to strengthen our faith.

Spiritual growth, much like the physical process, matures through normal stages. Various denominations and church traditions may call these stages by other names or emphasize them differently. Yet most people move through them in similar patterns. The process of spiritual growth involves at least four stages.

Stage 1—Prenatal Care

Before each of our three boys was born, we provided the best prenatal care possible. Their mother disciplined herself with a regimen of regular trips to the doctor, vitamins, and a strict diet. Mom and Dad prayed for each child's arrival and even played soft music to provide a calm, relaxed environment. Prenatal care is an important stage in the growth of a healthy newborn.

In a similar way, God the Father prepares for each child's birth into His family. He orchestrates (naturally or supernaturally) different events, people, and circumstances in the life of a "believer-to-be" in preparation for the person's "new birth." A good example of this can be found in 2 Timothy 1:5 and 2 Timothy 3:14-15 as Paul reflects on the process of how Timothy became a Christian. As you read this account of God's work in Timothy's life, it is important to note that even though Timothy's father was apparently absent, God provided other significant adult models in his life.

Stage 2—New Birth

Becoming a disciple of Jesus, or a member of God's family, begins with what Jesus called the "new birth." When Jesus told Nicodemus, a religious leader, that "no one can see the kingdom of God unless he is born again" (John 3:3), he meant that every person must be transformed into a child of God by the Spirit. Becoming a disciple (or Christian) is not a process of natural education or reformation whereby a person changes his or her beliefs and behaviors. It begins at a turning point in a person's life when one responds to God's invitation.

Jesus explained this turning point in different ways. In Matthew 18:3 He says, "unless you change and become like little children, you will never enter the kingdom of heaven." In Mark 10:21 Jesus says to a man preoccupied with his wealth, "Go, sell everything you have and give to the poor, and you will have treasure in heaven. Then come, follow me." To a teacher of the Jewish law Jesus responded to his inquiry about the greatest commandment by stating, "Love the Lord your God with all your heart and with all your soul and with all your mind and with all your strength," and "Love your neighbor as yourself" (Mark 12:30-31). Jesus phrased His invitations in various ways, depending on needs and reservations, and yet one theme is clear. Followers were asked to make a radical commitment to follow Him, thus allowing them to begin their pilgrimage with Jesus possessing a faith as small as a mustard seed. This small faith directed toward a powerful God accomplishes great things.

Phrases such as "becoming a Christian," "becoming Jesus' disciple," and "being born again" all refer to the same event—a supernatural work of God in a person's life that transforms him or her. This experience of conversion begins with a change in the heart, rooted in a person's emotions, intellect, and will. The transformation will take a lifetime to fully affect every aspect of one's life.

Stage 3—Becoming More Like Christ

Conversion brings immediate and instantaneous holiness as the new believer is now justified, credited as righteous, in the eyes of God. This has nothing to do with human goodness. It is totally based on Christ's sacrifice on the cross for sins. This is what Scripture records as being saved by grace (Rom. 3:22-26; 5:8; 8:1; Eph. 2:8-9). Paul makes clear in Romans 12:1-2 that sanctification, on the other hand, is a lifelong process of being changed into Christ's likeness.

The born-again believer has a supernatural desire to follow Jesus and obey His Word in response to God's grace. I have yet to see, however, a believer who lives in perfect obedience. If this were possible, we would not continue to need the sacrifice of Jesus (1 John 1:8-10). Walking in fellowship with the Lord means striving to live in obedience to His Word in everything we do, think, and say. To fail, intentionally or unintentionally, requires obedient confession of our sin to our Savior and claiming of His complete forgiveness.

The desire for instant spirituality or instant holiness, in practical experience, has led many Christians into despair or depression. There is no instant spiritual experience or secret doctrine that provides a shortcut to Christlikeness. The apostle Paul confessed he had not "already been made perfect" (Phil. 3:12). When Paul said this, he had been a Christian at least twenty-five years, completed three missionary journeys, and written nine of the New Testament epistles. Three verses later Paul includes himself among those who are "mature." He knew that maturity is never absolute. Growing toward Christlikeness is a life-long adventure.

Fortunately God has given us all the resources we need to live a victorious Christian life (2 Pet. 1:3) in the person, the power, and the gifts of the Holy Spirit. Just as the initial gift of the Holy Spirit revolutionized the early church, He wants to transform the hearts and lives of believers today. Most believers would confirm the fact that the Holy Spirit dwells in them, but some fail to experience the day-to-day reality of being "filled with the Spirit" (Eph. 5:18). In this text Paul commands believers to continually be filled with the Holy Spirit. Jesus told His disciples before He left that they would do even greater things than He did. The Holy Spirit plays the most significant role in enabling and empowering the new believer to become more like Jesus Christ (Rom. 15:16; Gal. 5:25; Eph. 3:16).

Stage 4—Becoming a Perfect Reflection of Christ

Some describe the disciple's life on earth as a pilgrimage to become more like Christ. There will be a time when the pilgrimage ends and the believer is transformed into the perfect likeness of Jesus (1 John 3:2). Theologians call this glorification. Paul foretold this event in Romans 8:29 when he said, "those God foreknew he also predestined to be conformed to the likeness of his Son." This final and complete transformation experience is the goal of the disciple's pilgrimage. Even though growing spiritually on earth may involve suffering, hardship, sacrifice, and failure, the final reward will be worth the struggle (Phil. 3:14). This ultimate prize of Christlikeness for all eternity should be the vision that keeps the Christian pilgrim focused throughout the earthly journey.

SUMMARY

Throughout church history, particularly in the midst of persecution, Christians have looked forward to the living hope of one day seeing Christ in glory. That hope carries with it the sure expectation of an inheritance that far surpasses the value of the greatest earthly treasure. The joy of eventually being like Christ and reflecting His radiant glory gives Christians a clear vision even in the midst of suffering, failure, and difficulty.

When Christ called men and women to follow Him, He never hid the cost. In fact, Jesus went out of His way to explain the radical nature of His standards for discipleship. But the cost was negligible compared to the glory to be revealed when His followers would actually become like their master. To become His disciple, Jesus taught that one's whole self must commit to loving and obeying Him.

The term *Christian* replaced the term *disciple* in the early church, and both terms initially implied radical commitments. But gradually the term *Christian* began to lose this distinctive biblical meaning. Nurturing the soul through at least four stages of spiritual development ultimately achieves a prize for the faithful follower of Jesus Christ.

FOR FURTHER DISCUSSION

1. What was your understanding of the difference in terminology between *Christian* and *disciple* before reading this chapter? How has it changed?

2. How do you react to the explanation of the possible reasons why the terms were exchanged?

3. Using today's language, how do you think Jesus would explain to someone how to become His follower?

4. In what ways does our future glorification give us hope in the midst of suffering?

3

The Church's Role in
Making Disciples

A FOUNDATIONAL COMPONENT of Jesus' strategy to make disciples is the role of the church, the body of Christ, in that process. Many people are not aware of the church as an organism, thinking only of its profile as an organization. In this chapter we discover the rich resources found in the universal church (Rom. 12:4-5) and manifested through local assemblies devoted to making disciples of Jesus.

THE GREAT COMMISSION AND THE CHURCH

At first glance, one might assume the Great Commission (Matt. 28:18-20) was directed to the eleven apostles rather than to the church. After all, the church was not even established when the challenge to "make disciples of all nations" was given. We learn in Acts 1:4, however, that just before the apostles were given this instruction, they were told not to do anything until the Holy Spirit came upon them. The initial command to make disciples was given to the eleven apostles, but the force that activated the Great Commission came to the whole church on the Day of Pentecost. As the mystery of the nature of the church is revealed by the New Testament writers, it becomes even more clear that the church is the primary recipient of the Great Commission and the body responsible to make disciples of Jesus Christ.

Terminology related to the word *disciple* that emerged between the 1960s through the 1980s camouflaged the role of the church even more. To "make disciples," or more commonly "to disciple," has often referred to a one-on-one (or small-group) relationship between an older and younger believer. Spiritual growth studies through the 1990s helped us understand the context of how the church functions as a unified body.

The Bible records many examples of mentor relationships between older and younger believers, but these are never referred to as "discipling" relationships. To view the biblical command to "make disciples" only through our contemporary concept of mentoring is to miss the major role of the church in fulfilling the Great Commission. Without minimizing the role individual Christians play in the process (as we will explore in chapter 7), their role must be seen as only a part of the Commission given to the universal body.

When Jesus gave the apostles the Great Commission of Matthew 28:18-20, the only command (in the original language) was to "make disciples." The other three verbs (going, baptizing, and teaching) are participles related to the major command. Examine the text in light of the grammatical structure just mentioned, and observe how significant the command "make disciples" is to the Great Commission. Jesus challenges His eleven apostles to make disciples of *Himself*—not disciples of Peter or Matthew or John. The Commission Jesus gave the eleven men (who had spent the last three years following Him) was to make people into disciples of Jesus Christ.

THE CHURCH AS THE BODY OF CHRIST

When Paul wrote about the nature of the church in Ephesians, he described it as the "body of Christ" (Eph. 1:22-23). Just as Christ nurtured His disciples while He was on earth, so Christ's body, the church, was to make His disciples after Pentecost. It is logical to assume that the church, as Christ's body, would have the authority to make disciples. The church, then, is key to fulfilling the Great Commission and helping believers grow toward spiritual maturity.

THE HOLY SPIRIT'S ROLE THROUGH THE CHURCH

The primary success factor for the Great Commission in the early church was the Holy Spirit. Before issuing the Great Commission, Jesus spent a great deal of time teaching about the role the Holy Spirit would play in the lives of followers after He left (John 14—16). Jesus strategically timed this teaching just prior to His arrest and crucifixion to show us how important the Holy Spirit's role would be in the growth of the church once Jesus physically departed. In one of their last meals together, Jesus commanded His disciples to wait until the Holy Spirit came before doing anything. The power, presence, and gifts of the Holy Spirit given to the church enabled the small band of disciples to accomplish an even broader ministry of discipleship than Christ Himself (John 14:12). While Jesus was on earth, His impact was limited to the scope of His personal ministry and the investment He made in training others.

There were obvious reasons why Christ told His leaders to wait until the coming of the Holy Spirit before beginning the task of the Great Commission. With Jesus in heaven, at the right hand of God the Father, they would have no one to guide them, empower them, and equip them for the task of making disciples. Although they had the words of Jesus carefully memorized and recorded, they were still severely limited without the supernatural work of the Holy Spirit. The Holy Spirit fulfilled Jesus' promise to provide needed resources.

The Power of the Holy Spirit

The power of the Holy Spirit was given to the church to empower its members, both individually and collectively, to be a witness. Today there is a renewed emphasis on the work of the Holy Spirit in individual lives, but there is little focus on the Holy Spirit's work within the church as a community. Interestingly, Luke writes: "When the day of Pentecost came, they were all together in one place" (Acts 2:1). When the Holy Spirit first came to the church, He came to the whole church, as a community. "All of them were filled with the Holy Spirit and began to speak in other tongues as the Spirit enabled them" (Acts 2:4). Certain leaders immediately emerged with the supernatural and more public gifts such as teaching, preaching, and miracles. The church as a Spirit-filled community played a major role in bringing disciples into the body of Christ.

After Peter's first public sermon after Pentecost, more than three thousand people became disciples (Acts 2:41). In the next paragraph (Acts 2:42-47), Luke records that the Holy Spirit's ministry resulted in a daily influx of new believers. The early church ministered to one another through their devotion to at least four regular practices: teaching, fellowship, the Lord's Supper, and prayer. They had close relationships with one another and shared sacrificially with people in need. Worship took place both in the temple and in homes where they also shared meals together. As a result of the radical nature of their spiritual community life, Luke reports that they won the support of those in the geographical community around them (Acts 2:47). The Holy Spirit transformed not only individual lives but also the whole community.

The church, through the supernatural resources of the Holy Spirit, was beginning its task of building disciples for Jesus.

Paul explains the connection between the power of the Holy Spirit and the ministry of the church in the world. In Paul's prayer (Eph. 1:15-23) for a local church, he asks that they may be "enlightened" to know the "incomparably great power for us who believe." He goes on to describe the nature of that power by comparing it to the power that raised Christ from the dead and seated Him at the right hand of the Father, far above all of Satan's power. Paul ends his prayer with a strong statement about the nature of the church in the world (vv. 22-23). Again in Ephesians 3:10, Paul states that God's "intent was that now, through the church, the manifold wisdom of God should be made known to the rulers and authorities in the heavenly realms." The church is God's divinely appointed means of impacting the world with the Gospel. The Holy Spirit empowers the church for this task.

The Presence of the Holy Spirit

Jesus foretold the coming of the Holy Spirit, "another Counselor," who would be with them forever. Jesus said that the Holy Spirit would be inside each of the disciples in a way they had never experienced before. He goes on to say, "I will not leave you as orphans; I will come to you. . . . On that day you will realize that I am in my Father, and you are in me, and I am in you" (John 14:16-20). He promised them that when the Holy Spirit came, they would experience a greater degree of intimacy with God through His presence within them. After Christ left the earth, He sent His presence in the person of the Holy Spirit to the church collectively and to each believer individually. In a real sense, the power of the Holy Spirit makes the church, as the community of disciples, the body of Christ. Since the presence of Christ Himself is found within the community of believers, the church as a community is uniquely able to make disciples of Jesus Christ.

The Gifts of the Holy Spirit

The gifts of the Holy Spirit uniquely enable the local church to be an ideal environment for disciples to grow and mature into Christlikeness. In Ephesians 4:7-8, Paul states, "to each one of us grace has been given as Christ apportioned it. This is why it says: 'When he ascended on high, he led captives in his train and gave gifts to men.'" Paul takes this illustration from a military custom. When an army conquered another city, the victors took prisoners back with them in a processional. As they entered their home city, the victorious army would distribute some of the spoils from the captured city as gifts to their people. Paul uses this illustration to explain the fact that when Jesus won the battle over Satan and his demons, through the power displayed in His resurrection, He took the highest place of authority and gave "gifts" to the church. These gifts of the Holy Spirit enable every believer to play a significant role in fulfilling the task of building disciples for Jesus Christ.

UNITY IN THE MIDST OF DIVERSITY FOSTERS MATURITY

If we picked friends who were all just like us, it might be fun for a while, but in time we would get bored. To grow and be challenged, we need to be around people who are different from us. Interestingly, Jesus designed the church to be made up of people from every tribe, culture, age group, and geographical location. It is the heterogeneous nature of the church that makes it such a rich environment in which to build disciples of Jesus Christ. If our goal is to make disciples of every nation, what better place to learn how to relate to people than in a local church fellowship? Within a local church setting we have the opportunity to interact with and learn from people of all ages, family backgrounds, income levels, and cultures. It is within the laboratory of the local church that disciples learn to love the way Christ loved.

DEVELOPING RELATIONSHIPS WITHIN THE CHURCH

Growth within the church (local and worldwide) depends on the quality of the relationships between believers. As the church follows biblical principles for interpersonal relationships, the local body of Christ will fulfill its mandate to be a greenhouse that nurtures disciples. Some of the major principles that guide interpersonal relationships in the church also challenge believers to edify, confess faults, forbear, empathize, submit to, accept, forgive, and admonish one another.

Edify One Another

The Bible uses the word *edify* to signify the process of building up and strengthening one another in the body of Christ (Eph. 4:16; Rom.

14:19; 1 Thess. 5:11). Ministry leaders must be able to build up the people they are working with because volunteers are motivated by intangible factors. Research among church volunteers indicates that the primary skill needed to motivate others in ministry is the ability to support and encourage.[1] Christians can do this through words of encouragement, notes of appreciation, gifts of fresh-baked cookies, and deeds of kindness. Simple tokens of encouragement like flowers or cards often say more than words.

Confess Faults to One Another

Christians, however committed they are to the Lord, are bound to make mistakes and hurt others' feelings. Whether it is forgetting an announcement, missing an appointment, or doing something foolish, we all make the occasional blunder. Even in our personal life, sin and mistakes happen. Sometimes it seems as if the older we get and the longer we walk with the Lord, the more aware we are of our shortcomings.

Yet the sign of a growing Christian is the ability to confess sin and deal with weaknesses courageously (1 John 1:8-10). By readily acknowledging weaknesses and sin, Christian leaders and teachers remain humble and teachable. Confessing faults to one another brings healing and keeps us accountable to other members of the body of Christ (Jas. 5:16).

Forbear with One Another

Christians, like all people, have personality quirks, weaknesses, bad habits, annoying mannerisms, and personal struggles. Within a close fellowship like the church these things easily become magnified by gossip and a judgmental spirit. As we bear patiently with offensive people, problems are often minimized (Eph. 4:2-3).

Empathize with One Another

Intelligence has been defined as the ability to think critically and quickly. Christians must add an interpersonal component to that definition to include the ability to see things from another person's point of view (Phil. 2:3-4). Empathizing with others means identifying with their feelings and showing compassion. Whether dealing with a sorrow or celebrating a success, people are built up when sincere members of the body come alongside to share these precious experiences with them (Gal. 6:2; Rom. 12:15).

Submit to One Another

Mutual submission is not a suggestion in Scripture; it is a command (Eph. 5:21). The supernatural strength to submit to others comes from being continually filled with the Holy Spirit (Eph. 5:18). The implication in Ephesians is that when Christians submit to the Holy Spirit's control, they will put the desires and wishes of others above their own. Practical implications of submission are discussed throughout Scripture in relation to spouses and partners, children and parents, slaves and masters, and citizens and government. The cultural context must be studied for direct application; however, the principle of mutual submission should characterize all relationships.

Accept One Another

There may be a tendency in some churches to become so passionate about advancing spiritual growth that they overlook those who grow at a different pace. Paul deals with this issue in Romans 14 and 15. He challenges believers to express their faith in different ways at the different stages of their walk with God. Such diversity enriches the church as a learning environment—a laboratory of interpersonal growth where Christians of all ages, stages, races, economic backgrounds, and cultures learn to love and accept one another as unique persons. Even though Jesus taught a high standard of discipleship, His followers displayed various degrees of commitment and maturity. It was His love and acceptance that compelled them all to higher levels of commitment.

Forgive One Another

Within such a diverse and complex community as the church, there will be times when other people hurt us, either intentionally or unintentionally. We must deal with the hurt in an appropriate way and forgive the offender. Jesus makes forgiving others a prerequisite for being forgiven by our heavenly Father (Matt. 6:14-15). As severe as this statement sounds, it gets to the heart of the gospel message. When we truly experience the forgiveness of Christ, we express that forgiveness to others. Christ, by example, did not always wait for the guilty person to repent (Luke 23:34; Eph. 4:32).

Some offensive behavior can simply be ignored and forgotten. Other behavior, especially when it negatively affects lives, needs to be tactfully confronted. If the guilty person asks for forgiveness, the problem resolves itself. If a person refuses to accept the responsibility for a sin, or perhaps blames someone else, the problem will usually intensify. If such a person displays a "hardened heart," we may be tempted to harbor bitter feelings. When Peter asked Jesus how many times he should forgive a person who had offended him, Jesus responded: "Not seven times, but seventy-seven times" (Matt. 18:22). If we are to continue to grow spiritually, we must never allow bitterness to take root in our hearts. We must be willing to forgive any person, no matter how deeply we have been hurt.

Admonish One Another

Just as love without discipline produces spoiled children, so encouragement without challenge produces weak saints. There are situations in the church where a soft approach will not work.

The word *admonish* means to challenge a person's thinking. It is usually distinguished from *teaching* because it implies that something needs to be changed. In order to admonish other believers to change significant issues in their lives, wisdom must be used (Col. 3:16). To be most effective, a good relationship needs to exist between all involved. Preferably the person doing the admonishing will be older and spiritually more mature. Respect is earned through godly character and a reputation for patient forbearance. That is why it is usually leaders, pastors, and teachers who are to admonish, rather than younger members of the body (1 Thess. 5:12). God's Word always provides the authoritative basis for admonishing others. If correction is done in the right way and with a humble spirit, most people appreciate the wise counsel.

SUMMARY

The Great Commission was given to the church as a body made up of many different types of people from all backgrounds and cultures. When the Holy Spirit was given to the church at Pentecost, His power, presence, and gifts enabled the early church to fulfill the Great Commission in ways never before imagined possible. As the church fulfills its task, the surrounding community feels the radical impact of Christian people. The health and unity of the church as a community must be continually developed if the church is to live up to its biblical mandate to make disciples of Jesus Christ.

FOR FURTHER DISCUSSION

1. In what ways is the church able to have a wider ministry of "making disciples" than even Jesus had?
2. What role does the Holy Spirit play in the lives of people in the church to enable them collectively to "make disciples" of Jesus?
3. Why are Spirit-directed interpersonal relationships so crucial to discipleship within the church?
4. In what ways should the church act as a greenhouse for growing disciples of Christ?
5. Why is the unity of the church central to the process of evangelism and discipleship?

4

Feasting on the Word

JUST AS NEWBORN INFANTS must drink milk to grow, so the new Christian must feed on the Word of God in order to grow and mature. Reading and studying God's Word provide the nourishment necessary for this growth (1 Pet. 2:2). While eating food may be only a routine of life for some people, God elevates the process of feeding on His Word to a feast. This feasting is described as delighting oneself, desiring gold, and eating honey. To grow and mature as disciples of Jesus, we must feed on God's Word as if it is exactly what it claims to be, the very Word of God Himself. The Word of God is the most concrete, objective Truth the disciple has to follow.

THE BIBLE AS GOD'S WORD

The Bible repeatedly claims to be God's Word. More than 760 times in the Old Testament the authors identify their messages as "the word of God" or some equivalent phrase. Hundreds of statements, especially in the Prophets, begin with some form of the expression "the Lord says" (e.g., Jer. 31:1-40). During His earthly ministry Jesus endorsed all three sections of the Hebrew Bible—the Law, the Prophets, and the Writings (Luke 24:44)—and emphasized the divine origin of the Old Testament (Mark 7:7-8).

The New Testament also claims to be God's Word. Jesus proclaimed His own gospel message with such divine authority (Matt. 7:28-29) that one astonished audience exclaimed, "No one ever spoke the way this man does" (John 7:46). Insisting that God was the source of His message, Jesus said, "I do nothing on my own but speak just what the Father has taught me" (John 8:28). The apostles also recognized the divine origin of their message and writings. Commending the Thessalonian believers, Paul wrote, "when you received the word of God, which you heard from us, you accepted it not as the word of men, but as it actually is, the word of God" (1 Thess. 2:13). Peter even gave Paul's epistles a scriptural status equal to the Old Testament (2 Pet. 3:16).

The Bible clearly claims to be God's Word. That claim is verified by Jesus, who demonstrated His own divine nature and trustworthiness by His sinless life, miracles, fulfillment of Old Testament prophecy, and, most of all, by His resurrection from the dead.

The Authority of God's Word

Because the Bible is God's Word, it demands serious attention and respect. Several terms explain the nature of this divine authority. Biblical *revelation* refers to the fact that God has taken the initiative to disclose information about His nature, eternal purposes, and provision for salvation in the words of Scripture. Much of this truth was not available apart from God's own communication of it (1 Cor. 2:6-12).

Biblical *inspiration* means that the Holy Spirit supernaturally controlled and guided the human authors of the biblical books so that they wrote precisely what God wanted said. As the human authors wrote from the background of their own experiences, using their minds and individual writing styles, they "spoke from God as they were carried along by the Holy Spirit" (2 Pet. 1:21). God's authorship of Scripture is not limited to passages where He is the direct speaker or dictated the contents. "All Scripture is God-breathed" (2 Tim. 3:16). Even the choice of individual words was divinely controlled so that the terms used would convey the right meaning.

Biblical *infallibility* refers to the effectiveness of God's Word in achieving God's intended purposes (Isa. 55:11). God so works through the biblical message that His intentions are accomplished.

Biblical *inerrancy* is a technical phrase for the accuracy of the biblical message. It affirms that what the Bible teaches on any subject it addresses is true. Properly understood, the message of the Bible gives correct information (Heb. 2:1-4).

Ultimately the authority of God's Word focuses on personal accountability. God enforces His message (Heb 2:1-4). Growing spiritually requires responding to the biblical message with undivided attention, humble submission, and unqualified obedience (Jas. 1:19-22).

The Unity of God's Word

Although the Bible contains sixty-six different books written over a period of approximately 1,500 years, it holds together as the ongoing story of God's redemptive program in the world. The Old Testament focuses primarily on God's dealing with His people Israel. The New Testament continues the story with the founding of the church, composed of believers in Jesus from every nation. God has not forgotten His promises to Israel. His blessing focused on the church after Pentecost to show the breadth of His mercy. A continuity of promise and fulfillment links the two Testaments (Matt. 5:17). The future age of spiritual blessing, predicted by the prophets, began with the ministry of Jesus (Luke 4:16-21). Even the Gentile outreach of the church is the achievement of God's initial promise to Abraham that "all peoples on earth will be blessed through you" (Gen. 12:3 with Gal. 3:8).

Consequently, believers are biblical Christians, not just New Testament Christians. Insights for spiritual growth and Christian living come from the whole Bible (Rom. 15:4; 1 Cor. 10:6-11). God's supernatural control insures a coherent, noncontradictory biblical message.

The Clarity of God's Word

One does not have to be a seminary professor or even a pastor to know what the Bible means. Scripture was not written to confuse or conceal, but to clearly communicate God's message. God's truth was told in languages spoken in everyday life. "Setting forth the truth plainly" (2 Cor. 4:2) was a conscious objective of Paul's ministry. Except for a few obvious exceptions, biblical authors wrote to be understood.

The Bible as a Catalyst for Growth

The Bible uses several picture words from everyday life to show the great variety of ways in which God's Word helps the believer to grow. As seed, God's Word is the source of growth (Matt. 13:1-26). Young Christians grow spiritually because they are well nourished by the food God's Word provides (1 Pet. 2:2). Using the Bible as a mirror enables believers to evaluate the consistency of their Christian living (Jas. 1:22-25). When Satan attacks God's people, God's Word serves as "the sword of the Spirit," the offensive weapon that defeats the enemy (Eph. 6:17). Like light illuminating a dark path, biblical principles provide guidance in daily decision-making (Ps. 119:105). God's Word is a tremendous resource for Christian growth and living.

One of the most important purposes of the Word of God is explained in Hebrews 4:12: "The word of God is living and active. Sharper than any double-edged sword, it penetrates even to dividing soul and spirit, joints and marrow; it judges the thoughts and attitudes of the heart." When this verse is examined within the context of the previous two chapters, it clearly indicates that God's Word keeps believers from getting a hard heart. Reflective study of God's Word keeps the Christian's heart moldable and responsive to God's voice. A soft heart provides the richest soil for the seed of God's Word to grow.

The Bible as a Ministry Training Manual

After declaring the divine inspiration of Scripture, Paul makes a surprisingly bold statement in 2 Timothy 3:16-17. He says that all Scripture is "useful for teaching, rebuking, correcting and training in righteousness, so that the man of God may be thoroughly equipped for every good work." The Bible must be our foundational truth for learning how to grow and minister. Other resources that aid the process of growing and reaching out to others must always be tested against the foundational principles of Scripture.

PRINCIPLES FOR STUDYING THE BIBLE

Knowing how valuable God's Word is for spiritual growth, believers should read the Bible with intense personal interest. After all, the ultimate purpose of studying Scripture is to relate biblical truth to daily living. Followers of Christ are obligated to do more than just study the Word. They are to obey it (Jas. 1:22).

It is grossly inappropriate to try to apply a passage of Scripture directly to our lives today without studying what it meant within its original historical and cultural context. By following these three steps of Bible study, we can be confident we are accurately handling God's Word (2 Tim. 2:15).

1. Observation
2. Interpretation
3. Application

Step 1—Observation

Observation focuses on what the passage says. At this step the reader watches for all the important facts. Someone has well said, "If you look for nothing, you will find it every time." Most important information will be discovered by looking for the five "W's" and an "H" used by journalists: *who, what, when, where, why,* and *how.* Observe all these details using a concordance or word study book to look up the meanings of words and note how they are used in other parts of the Bible.

Finally in the observation step, organize the main points of the text or story into a logical outline. This will help to identify the pattern of the thought processes of the author and the big idea of the text.

Step 2—Interpretation

Interpretation asks what the passage means. All the details previously observed in the passage are now analyzed to discover the point the author was trying to make. One must study important words, significant grammatical relationships, and relevant background information using Bible dictionaries and commentaries to find their precise meanings. The correct understanding of the passage adequately accounts for all of these facts. If some information does not fit naturally with the explanation of the passage, the interpretation needs revision.

Hermeneutics is the science of determining the correct rules to follow when interpreting the Bible. Examine how the people used language to communicate ideas. The main idea of most passages is clear from a simple reading of the text. Others require careful thought to get to the author's point (2 Pet. 3:16). It is easy to twist Scripture to make it support our own biases. Most cults are based on misinterpreted biblical passages. Carefully study, using correct rules, to avoid distorting God's Word (2 Cor. 4:2).

The Bible was originally written in foreign languages to people living a long time ago in another part of the world with a different culture. A study process for God's Word is more necessary now than it was for the original recipients in biblical times. The following rules of hermeneutics help us overcome barriers to understanding.

READ FOR THE MAIN IDEA OF THE PARAGRAPH

Bible reading should seek to discover the main point of each paragraph. Paragraphs, not verses, are the focus of good reading. Each paragraph consists of several sentences on the same subject. The main idea of the paragraph is the central theme that holds the verses together. Having identified this main idea, the reader is able to determine how each sentence helps the author make his point. Stating the main idea of the paragraph in one concise sentence may be hard at first, but it gets easier with practice.

Modern verse divisions added in A.D. 1560 are both a blessing and a curse. Without them, it would be next to impossible to find a specific passage. But with them, people treat each verse as an independent unit of thought. Trying to understand a verse apart from its paragraph makes it easy to insert one's own ideas in error. What the author meant by a verse is clear only when it is explained consistently with the main idea of its paragraph. A wise principle of Bible study warns: The shorter the passage interpreted, the greater the danger of error.

IDENTIFY THE AUTHOR'S LITERARY STYLE

Whenever you hear someone complain about a speaker by saying, "Did he ever dig himself into a hole!" your first impulse is not to look for a ladder to help him get out. The word *hole* in this sense does not mean a pit in the ground. It is a way of saying that his excessive argument was inconsistent. Similarly, biblical authors often used figures of speech. The historical books and New Testament epistles were written in a fairly direct style. Old Testament prophets often used poetry, like those who composed psalms and proverbial sayings. Jesus frequently taught in parables that are figurative stories, illustrating deep truths or abstract concepts. Each literary style uses language in a special way. Readers must understand every passage according to its distinct literary style.

CONSIDER THE FLOW OF THE BIBLICAL CONTENT

In normal conversation, we understand words and sentences according to their context. Thoughts are expressed by a series of related ideas. Accurate Bible reading requires understanding what is written according to the author's train of thought. Specific phrases and sentences must be understood in a way consistent with the author's main idea. For example, the promise of wisdom in James 1:5 does not guarantee risk-free decision-making through prayer. Earlier in the paragraph, James tells believers to respond with joy to hardships in life because endurance of difficult experiences develops spiritual maturity. Here the promised wisdom provides insight on how to cope during the hard experience.

UNDERSTAND THE MEANING OF KEY WORDS

Words express ideas, but many words have several different meanings. The statement, "That was the largest trunk I had ever seen" can mean more than one thing. Does "trunk" refer to a tree, car, elephant, suitcase, or clothing? Normally, the other ideas mentioned in the context automatically make clear which meaning the author had in mind. Similarly, when people read the Bible from a good modern language translation, the meaning of most words will be clear. Important words or unclear terms need to be researched. Often shades of a word's meaning are difficult for a translation to suggest but add much insight to the author's intent. Carefully select the best meaning for each word in light of the words actually used by the author. For example, students often inappropriately claim the promise of "wisdom" in James 1:5 when they take tests. What they need is "knowledge," not "wisdom." Quoting this verse is no substitute for study.

FOLLOW THE FORCE OF THE GRAMMAR

Normally people communicate with a series of words. One-word sentences are rare. The way words are arranged in a sentence affects their meaning as much as the choice of the words. To say, "The man hit the ball," is quite different from, "The ball hit the man." The reader must pay close attention to grammatical forms used to communicate the author's point.

When James commands his readers to "consider it pure joy" (Jas. 1:2) when they experience different kinds of adversity, he is not suggesting that they convince themselves the situation is not so bad. Rather, by beginning verse 3 with the word *because*, James shows the reason why believers are to respond to adversity with joy. They know that the trying of their faith produces perseverance, a much needed spiritual quality.

VIEW FROM HISTORICAL PERSPECTIVE

Reading the Bible is like reading someone else's mail. To understand God's message to another continent, an earlier century, and a different culture, the reader needs to know as much as possible about the circumstances. The more readers mentally place themselves in the situation of the original audience, the better they are able to know the intended meaning and its significance for today.

INTEGRATE WITH OTHER BIBLICAL TEACHING ON THE SUBJECT

The Bible does not say all it has to say about a subject in any one passage. Information learned in one passage should be understood in conjunction with other key verses on the same subject. Basing an action on only one verse is like running with only one shoe on.

Step 3—Application

Application determines the relevance of the message for God's people living today. The whole Bible is God's Word; however, it includes some cultural things God does not necessarily expect believers to practice today. Four specific guidelines help the believer determine what is valid for today:

• First, biblical statements that are universal in scope have timeless relevance. These will be expressed in general terms as true for all believers. Conversely, commands given to an individual in some specific situation usually apply only to that person. Universals will be based on Christian truth rather than on cultural factors. Sometimes doctrine requires a certain quality of response, and the local culture will determine the specific physical expression.

• Second, promises that are conditional only apply when the condition is met.

• Third, guidelines changed by later revelation no longer apply. The dietary and sacrificial regulations of the Old Testament have been removed by the finished work of Christ.

• Fourth, biblical examples are relevant to the extent that they are approved or censured by the biblical authors. Just because an act is recorded in the Bible does not make the act right.

SUMMARY

The main ingredient for spiritual growth is a steady diet of God's Word. The steps in studying the Bible accurately include observation, interpretation, and application. By following proper hermeneutical principles under the illumination of the Holy Spirit, we can be confident that we are getting our direction from God rather than from our own imag-ination. Our goal should go beyond just *doing* Bible study to actually feasting on God's Word daily and applying it to our lives.

FOR FURTHER DISCUSSION

1. What evidence is there that the Bible claims to be God's Word?
2. Discuss how biblical revelation, inspiration, infallibility, and inerrancy differ from each other. Why are they important?
3. Explain why the unity of the Bible is so surprising. Describe what holds the message of the Bible together.
4. Why are rules necessary for Bible study?

5

Developing Intimacy
with God

IT WOULD BE HARD to imagine a healthy marriage relationship where a husband and wife did not talk to one another on a regular basis. Yet it is even more impossible to comprehend how people could claim to know God without talking to Him regularly. The key to intimacy with God is through a disciplined, regular pattern of communication with Him through prayer.

While godly people in Scripture approached God in prayer in various ways, the one common characteristic was that they put a priority on prayer. Daniel made it his practice to pray three times a day. David prayed through psalms and music. Jesus, even though He was fully God, made communication with His Father an absolute priority. His pattern was to rise early in the morning, before dawn, to talk to the Father. Before all major decisions, He spent lengthy times in solitude and prayer. Paul continues this priority in both his practice and teaching. He is an example to all of us in his practice of continually praying for people and situations. His letters include some of the richest prayers in Scripture.

The biblical record indicates a variety of postures in prayer. Kneeling, lying prostrate, raising arms, and even dancing before the Lord reflect the diversity of expression in prayer. People pray loudly, quietly, in unknown languages, through musical instruments, and in singing. The issue in prayer is not necessarily how prayer is done, but rather the source of the communication. While prayer from the heart of a person seems to touch the heart of God, external prayers that have no personal meaning do not seem to make any connection. God desires His children to draw close to Him through prayer. Through prayer, we tap into the resources that God has for us to grow into His likeness.

PURPOSEFUL PRAYER

Knowing why we need to pray may spark us to become more deliberate and passionate in our prayer life. So why pray? Since God is all-knowing, all-powerful, and all-loving, what purpose does prayer serve? Certainly, prayer is not needed to inform God about personal circumstances. God knows what His people need before they ask (Matt. 6:32). Likewise, it is not necessary for people to try to change God's attitude toward them. God is not a cosmic bully intent on harming people. Although pagan prayers often were designed to appease a hostile deity, the true God does not desire appeasement (Matt 6:25-34). After all, God gives only good gifts (Jas. 1:17).

Furthermore, prayer is not talking God into something that He does not want to do. The Christian's proper attitude in prayer is submission to God's will, not achieving his or her own (Matt. 6:10). Jesus' prayer as He awaited His impending crucifixion makes this clear: "My Father, if it is possible, may this cup be taken from me. Yet not as I will, but as you will" (Matt. 26:39). The believer's assurance in prayer is, "if we ask anything according to his will, he hears us" (1 John 5:14).

The purpose of prayer is not to change God's mind. Rather, it is to align one's will with God's will. Passages where God appears to modify His stated plans in response to prayer probably were learning experiences designed by God to teach valuable lessons to His children (Gen. 18:16-33).

If prayer does not do any of these things, it seems like a complete waste of time and effort! Why pray? Because God has willed to work in answer to prayer. Prayer makes a difference. "The prayer of a righteous man is powerful and effective" (Jas. 5:16). Prayer becomes a powerful means by which the follower of Jesus Christ utilizes the resources of God to further His kingdom here on earth.

Someone has well said, "Prayer is for our benefit, not God's." Being sovereign over everyone and everything that exists, God does not need human prayer to accomplish His eternal purposes. Yet He chose prayer to be the vehicle He would use to deliver His blessings to His children. Prayer unlocks the door to the storehouse of God's riches.

COMPONENTS OF A RICH PRAYER LIFE

When we study Scripture as a whole, we find several aspects of prayer that characterize godly men and women with rich prayer lives: worship, confession, adoration, praise, thanksgiving, intercession, and requests.

Worship

Entering God's presence should impress believers with His worth. A sense of awe and reverence is the natural response to the presence of the greatest being there is. When believers meditate on who God is, a feeling of esteem for God fills their hearts. By concentrating on the perfection of God's being, believers clear their minds of the clutter from daily life that distracts them from sensing God's presence. Because God is spirit, He desires that His children worship Him "in spirit and in truth" (John 4:23-24). God must be valued above all else as we approach Him in prayer.

Confession

Recognition of God's holiness naturally leaves people with a sense of sinfulness, requiring confession. Experiencing how utterly holy God is, the prophet Isaiah cried out, "Woe to me! I am ruined! For I am a man of unclean lips, and I live among a people of unclean lips, and my eyes have seen the King, the LORD Almighty" (Isa. 6:5). Every believer needs this cleansing that comes from acknowledging guilt. "If we confess our sins, he is faithful and just and will forgive us our sins and purify us from all unrighteousness" (1 John 1:9). This means that God is absolutely right in forgiving sin every time believers truly confess. People often stop growing spiritually because they fail to accept God's forgiveness. A healthy prayer life is an antidote to spiritual paralysis.

Adoration

Reassured by the loving forgiveness of the heavenly Father (1 John 4:10), believers need to tell God how much they love Him. An atmosphere of adoration and affectionate warmth marks a good prayer time. Expressing love to God by word and obedient actions is the only appropriate response to one who loves believers so much (1 John 3:1; 4:16). Jesus taught that our first responsibility is to love God with our whole being (Matt. 22:37). This love is no empty sentimental gesture. It reflects the resolve of the will as well as the emotions.

Praise

Whereas worship appreciates who God is, praise pays tribute to what God does. He deserves praise "for his acts of power . . . for his surpassing greatness" (Ps. 150:2). Believers should speak highly of His great goodness and gracious compassion (Ps. 145:4-9). Because "the LORD is good to all; he has compassion on all he has made" (Ps. 145:9). God is honored, and Christians grow when they credit Him. Praise projects a positive outlook on life by remembering God's favors.

Thanksgiving

No aspect of prayer is more essential than thanksgiving. Having received God's forgiving grace and sustaining strength, Christians owe Him a deep sense of gratefulness. Ingratitude lies at the heart of rebellion against God (Rom. 1:21). In arrogant pride people ignore God, choosing rather to credit themselves for the blessings of life. This ungrateful attitude has no place among believers. Thanksgiving is an attitude for all seasons. Hard times are as much an occasion for gratitude as good times (1 Thess. 5:18). Even experiences that normally cause tension are to be faced with thankful prayer, anticipating inward peace (Phil. 4:6-7). Knowing that God is in control and will use this hardship to promote spiritual growth is sufficient reason to pray thankfully (Rom. 8:28; Jas. 1:2-4).

Intercession

Prayer is also a time to ask God to meet the needs of others. The phrase "God first, others second, self last" applies well to prayer. Paul regularly prayed for the spiritual maturity of believers (Phil. 1:9-11; Eph. 1:16-23; 3:14-21) and asked them to pray for his consistent witness (Eph. 6:18-20). Through prayer you can contribute positively to the lives of others way beyond the limits of your personal resources and capacities (Phil. 1:19).

Requests

Finally, prayer is telling God all the details of everything that concerns you (Phil. 4:6). Seeking help from God for personal challenges, problems, and opportunities is not selfish. Jesus encouraged His disciples to take their requests to God in His name (John 16:23-24). Through prayer you receive divine help for daily needs.

PRAYER RESULTS

Prayer played a vital part in the lives of God's people in biblical times. The Old Testament leaders Abraham, Moses, Nehemiah, Ezra, godly

Job, and Hannah; the prophets Samuel, Elijah, Elisha, Jonah, Daniel, and Jeremiah; and the kings David, Solomon, and Hezekiah all witnessed God's direct involvement in their lives through prayer. Although Jesus was God, during His life on earth He prayed regularly to His heavenly Father. Following His teaching, the apostles and later the early church placed a priority on prayer. In all these cases, God followed no single pattern in responding to His people's requests. Whether the loving divine answer was "yes," "wait," or "no," prayer greatly affected their lives and the lives of others.

Granting of Requests

In the Old Testament numberless examples of how God grants requests are found. Israel's early leaders knew the power of prayer. When Abraham prayed for Abimelech, king of Gerar, the king's life was spared, and his wife was able to have children again (Gen. 20:17-18). Several times during the wilderness wanderings, Moses prayed for the rebellious Israelites, and God spared them from threatened destruction (Num. 11:2; 14:12-16; 21:7).

The history of the nation Israel was one of recurring defection from God, divine discipline, and prayer-secured deliverance. After the people repented for their idolatry, God broke the Philistine dominance over them in answer to Samuel's prayer (1 Sam. 7:5-13). Later, when Saul became Israel's first king, Samuel showed God's displeasure at their wanting a king like other nations by praying down a thunderstorm. In spite of Israel's sin, Samuel also prayed for their well-being (1 Sam. 12:16-23).

When David and Solomon reigned over the united kingdom, Israel was led by men of prayer. Many psalms are prayers of David (Ps. 17; 72; 86; 142). David's confession of his sin with Bathsheba is a pattern for all subsequent generations (Ps. 51). Solomon's prayer for wisdom at his coronation (1 Kings 3:7-9) and humility in his prayer dedicating the temple brought divine blessing on the whole nation (1 Kings 8:22-53).

In the New Testament prayer continues its crucial role. During His earthly ministry, Jesus' prayers were directly connected with the descent of the Holy Spirit upon Him at His baptism (Luke 3:21-22), times of heavy ministry (Mark 1:35; Luke 5:16), the selection of the disciples (Luke 6:12), the confession by Peter that He was "the Christ of God" (Luke 9:18-20; Matt. 16:16), His transfiguration on the mountain (Luke 9:29), and His betrayal and crucifixion (Luke 22:40-44).

Through prayer the early church received guidance in the choice of an apostle to replace Judas (Acts 1:24), courage to witness during times of persecution (Acts 4:31), the initial outpouring of the Holy Spirit on Samaritan believers (Acts 8:15), God's orders to reach out to Gentiles (Acts 10:9-23), divine initiation and enablement for Paul's missionary journeys (Acts 13:1-3), the appointment of local church leaders (Acts 14:23), and release from prison (Acts 12:12; 16:25-40). God guided, equipped, and enabled the early church for effective ministry in response to the prayers of godly disciples.

Delaying Until a Better Time

Even in biblical times God did not always answer His people's requests immediately. Sometimes God waited for His right time. The heavens seemed closed to the cries of Job as his family's circumstances went from bad to worse. But God's answer was not "no." By delaying the end of Job's suffering, God taught His servant valuable spiritual lessons that could only be learned in adversity. Ultimately Job emerged as a more mature child of God with restored health and doubled finances (Job 3:11-23; 7:20; 42:8-10; Jas. 5:11). Married couples unable to have children waited and yearned and waited again, despairing of ever having a family. In God's perfect time Hannah conceived her son Samuel (1 Sam. 1:5-7, 20), and Elizabeth and Zechariah bore John the Baptist (Luke 1:13).

Affirming a Superior Way

At times the believer's wiser heavenly Father lovingly denies a request because He knows what is best for His begging child. Only a cruel parent would have granted Elijah's (1 Kings 19:4) or Jonah's (Jonah 4:1-10) prayers for death. Being depressed, the prophets were not thinking clearly, and so God said, "no." Death was no solution for prophets who had just been God's instruments for revival.

Often God denied a specific request not because it was foolish or bad, but because He had something better in mind. Paul's "thorn in the flesh" is an example of this. On three separate occasions Paul "pleaded with the Lord to take it away." God refused but assured Paul, "My grace is sufficient for you, for my power is made perfect in weakness" (2 Cor. 12:7-10). Paul discovered that the spiritual blessing supplied by God's grace in times of adversity far surpassed any inconvenience or pain.

Definite Answers to Prayer

Testimonies abound to God's faithful answers to the requests of His children. Believers imprisoned for their faith report receiving courage and spiritual strength when they prayed. Some suffering from serious life-threatening illnesses have been miraculously healed because God's people prayed. The church has grown in nations where Christianity is illegal or suppressed in answer to the prayers of foreign believers not even allowed in those countries. Lives wrecked by sin and drugs have been transformed by conversion experiences that have come after years of faithful prayer by relatives or close friends. Many rejoice in the multitude of daily needs for which God specifically provides through the prayers of the saints.

Realistic Expectations in Prayer

Believers often experience frustration when they do not see direct results from their prayers. Some accuse God of not keeping His Word, when in reality they have misunderstood His promises concerning prayer. Jesus' promise that the Father would give "whatever" His disciples asked (John 16:23-24) must not be taken to mean that God will always do precisely what believers want. Prayer is a request to God for help, not a demand for action. The John 16 passage contains a proverbial type promise that states a general truth without indicating any qualifications or exceptions. Other passages make it clear that requests motivated by selfish desire (Jas. 4:3) or opposed to God's will are not answered (1 John 5:14). Answers to prayer are not some kind of demand performance by God. He is not under any contractual obligation to give everything His people want. God evaluates every prayer by His infinite wisdom and unfailing love. He gives only what He knows is best.

Some believe that the answer is guaranteed when two people agree, failing to realize that this promise has to do with church discipline, not prayer for things (Matt. 18:19). This passage deals with reconciliation and forgiveness. The agreement concerns the kind of discipline that God should bring upon an unrepentant guilty party. It is dangerous to give false expectations based on misunderstanding Scripture. When prayers are not answered positively, people feel that God has failed them. They become disappointed in God for something He never promised to do.

Confident Assurance in Prayer

From a limited human perspective, there seems to be no value in experiencing disease, hardships, adversity, and persecution. Given the option, Christians would veto the invasion of these experiences into their lives. Yet these problems are a part of the sinful, fallen world in which both believers and nonbelievers live. God hates these terrible results of the Fall and has acted decisively, defeating Satan, who has the power of death (Heb. 2:14). Knowing that God "is able to do immeasurably more than all we ask or imagine, according to his power that is at work within us" (Eph. 3:20), believers should pray with confidence. Nothing is too hard for God.

Yet while God promises to come to the aid of His children in these hard circumstances, He never promises us freedom from such difficulties. In fact, Jesus clearly warns His disciples that they will have tribulation in this world. He offers peace within these crises, not immunity from them (John 16:33). As in biblical times, God sometimes chooses to glorify His name by miraculously removing the problem; at other times He strengthens believers so that they can persevere to God's glory. Anytime God chooses not to heal sickness or remove a difficult problem, His children should rest in confident assurance that God is working His plan out under His ultimate control. The fact that we do not understand does not mar either God's love or His character but simply reflects the fact that we see things from a limited earthly perspective.

As we discussed in chapter 1, some of our most valuable learning experiences happen within the context of challenge, suffering, and stress. The key to passing the test in these situations is in the depth of our trusting relationship with Jesus Christ. While such crises can draw us into a more intimate walk with the Lord, it is much wiser to be prepared ahead of time for the inevitable storms in life by fostering an intimate prayer life with the Father during the good times.

SUMMARY

Prayer is the catalyst in growing toward spiritual maturity. Through prayer, the believer draws on the riches of God's blessing and power. Yet God is not a spiritual Santa Claus. While He listens to the prayers of His children, He does not always answer us in the way that we might want. His highest purpose for prayer is to usher us into His presence. For this reason a rich prayer life should include all of these elements: worship, confession, adoration, praise, thanksgiving, intercession, and requests. A preoccupation with prayer merely as a means to get what we want is a sign more of carnality than spirituality. Spiritual maturity is evidenced by both an intimate prayer life and a humble submission to the sovereign will of God.

FOR FURTHER DISCUSSION

1. Name three things prayer does not do, and explain why in each case.
2. Since prayer does not do these things, why pray?
3. If Jesus was fully God, why did He have to spend so much time in prayer?
4. Why is it wrong to think that prayer guarantees you will get everything you request?
5. How can "wait" or "no" be viewed as positive answers to prayer?
6. Discuss definite answers to prayer that you, your family, or church have received this past month.
7. Identify some false expectations people have concerning prayer, and discuss why these are a serious problem.

6

Establishing a Godly Lifestyle

CHRISTIANS WHO WANT to grow spiritually will impact the world only to the degree that they live what they say they believe. Holiness is not an option for the growing Christian. It is a prerequisite for service in the kingdom of God. A pure heart is required for servants of a holy God.

Yet God does not require moral perfection from His disciples. One only has to look at the heroes of the faith, recorded in Hebrews 11, to see that God uses men and women in spite of their imperfections. The fact, however, that God can use weak and sinful people to accomplish His plans does not give believers an excuse to live in sin. Rather, it should challenge them to get rid of the sin in their lives and press on in the race of faith (Heb. 12:1-2).

Holiness is not merely living up to some superficial human standard of perfection. Holiness is an attitude of the heart that expresses itself in godly living. A holy, godly lifestyle must first cultivate a heart for God; second, overcome temptation; and third, establish patterns of holy living.

CULTIVATE A HEART FOR GOD

Godliness is an attitude of the heart that radiates through godly behavior. The word *heart* throughout Scripture portrays the whole inner life, including the mind, emotions, and will. The Holy Spirit desires to fill our hearts with His supernatural presence. As the heart is filled up with God, it overflows into words, actions, and godly behavior.

Open Up to God

God has never been satisfied with superficial service and worship. Religious activity is futile unless it comes from the heart (Isa. 29:13).

God has commanded that His people love Him with their whole beings—heart, mind, soul, and might (Deut. 6:5; Matt. 22:37). In order to do so, believers must allow the Spirit of God to penetrate every area of their inner lives.

Likewise, if we are to continue to grow and mature as Christians, we must allow the Spirit of God to break up the hard areas in our hearts (Jer. 4:3-4). We must cultivate a tender heart for God.

Confess Your Sin to God

Once we have opened up the secret and hidden places of our hearts to God, we must confess specific sins to Him (1 John 1:9). The simple, humble confession of sin before God opens the door of forgiveness, healing, and power for the believer. The power of the almighty God is activated in humble hearts, sensitive to the conviction of the Holy Spirit (Isa. 57:15). To continue to grow spiritually, we must develop the daily practice of examining our heart and actions before God and confessing known sin.

Desire the Fullness of the Holy Spirit

Once a person has dealt ruthlessly with known sin, one needs to fill that emptiness with the fullness of the Holy Spirit. The Holy Spirit empowers the Christian for service. He was given to the church, in part, to empower it to witness (Acts 1:8). Believers are commanded to continue to be filled with the Holy Spirit (Eph. 5:18).

Throughout the Old Testament, believers are compelled to seek God. As the psalmist states: "As the deer pants for streams of water, so my soul pants for you, O God. My soul thirsts for God, for the living God. When can I go and meet with God?" (Ps. 42:1-2).

What was experienced only periodically by people of God in the Old Testament is now a permanent gift to the church in the New Testament. Jesus, in reference to the gift of the Holy Spirit, quotes Isaiah 44:3: "Streams of living water will flow from within him" (John 7:38). As these and other Scriptures indicate, the Holy Spirit not only fills people's hearts but also flows out into the lives of others. By being filled with the Holy Spirit, believers receive power to witness, reflecting the fullness of God through their lifestyles.

Establishing a godly lifestyle begins with cultivating a heart for God. It demands discipline and perseverance in maintaining a daily time of reflection, Bible study, and prayer. By writing reflections, concerns, and prayers in a journal, the serious follower of Christ can keep accountable to God for personal growth.

OVERCOME TEMPTATION

Growing Christians are often even more susceptible to temptation than unbelievers. Just because a person is committed to being used by God does not mean he or she is sheltered from Satan's schemes. It may even mean that Satan will fight harder to bring such a person into temptation. In order to have an exemplary, godly lifestyle, we must learn how to overcome temptation.

There are three practical ways to overcome temptation: First, admit your weaknesses; second, use God's resources; and third, guard your thought life.

Admit Your Weaknesses

Some believers, in an attempt to keep a good image in front of others, act as if they never struggle with sin or temptation. They often feel that if they share their struggles, they will come across as being weak. Yet Scripture reveals a different model of the "ideal Christian." The power of the Holy Spirit seems to be activated in believers' lives when they are humbly aware of their own weaknesses. When Christians get too confident and proud, they are more apt to depend on their own talents and abilities and leave God out. To grow spiritually we must be willing to admit our weaknesses, sins, struggles, and failures.

Use God's Resources

The psalmist makes a direct connection between his weakness and God's strength in Psalm 73:26: "My flesh and my heart may fail, but God is the strength of my heart and my portion forever." The power of God is unleashed when we humbly depend on Him for strength in the midst of human weakness. God's resources are available to overcome temptation. God promises that as we draw near to Him, He will draw closer to us. As we approach God with a humble heart, He promises to give us the needed resources to overcome temptation (Jas. 4:7-10).

In Ephesians 6:10-20, Paul refers to some of God's resources as the "armor of God." Defensively he challenges Christian soldiers to protect themselves with truth, righteousness, the message of the gospel of peace, faith, and salvation. Offensively he challenges believers to arm themselves with the Word of God and persistent prayer.

Finally, the growing Christian should wield God's Word to silence the accusations of Satan and to shed light on the path ahead. Through these resources God makes it possible for us to overcome temptation.

Guard Your Thought Life

Sin comes from the heart (Matt. 15:18). Any strategy to overcome temptation must begin with the heart. If a sinful thought or desire is not dealt with immediately, it may lead to sinful behavior. When Christians fall, it usually is because they have allowed sinful thoughts and desires to burn unrestrained in their hearts over a period of time. The way to overcome such temptations is to learn to discipline thoughts.

Paul, in his explanation of how he avoided falling into Satan's schemes, states that "we take captive every thought to make it obedient to Christ" (2 Cor. 10:5). In order to continue to grow and mature in Christ, we must guard our hearts from any thought or desire that would violate scriptural principles or laws.

By dealing ruthlessly with sin at the thought level, we dampen the spark that could ignite into a sinful action. At the first indication of a tempting thought, it may help to quote an appropriate Scripture verse or sing a hymn softly. By turning our thoughts to God, we will receive deliverance from temptation.

ESTABLISHING PATTERNS OF HOLY LIVING

To continue to grow as disciples of Jesus, our lifestyle must be consistent with biblical principles of holiness. While establishing a godly lifestyle begins in the heart, its evidence is seen in daily behavior. Godly actions and deeds spring from a pure heart and disciplined lifestyle. In order to establish patterns of holy living, we must first maintain biblical standards; second, discipline all areas of our life; and third, be accountable to other Christians.

Maintain Biblical Standards

God commands Christians to be holy and blameless in their behavior simply because of the fact that He is holy (1 Pet. 1:15; Lev. 11:44). In order to grow more like Christ, we must strive to be like Him in His holiness.

The standard of holiness must be God's standard—perfect holiness. Rather than adopt the standards of morality practiced in the world or even in the church, the growing Christian must continually seek to live up to God's principles and standards of holiness found in His Word.

The fact that believers will always fall short of God's perfect standard should not discourage us but rather drive us to the cross. There is no need for Christians to feel condemned for falling short of God's standard of holiness (Rom. 8:1). Through the blood of Christ, believers are made holy by an act of God (Gal. 3:2-3).

Our striving to live up to biblical standards of holiness, however, is not in order to earn God's favor or to appease His wrath but rather as a heartfelt response to His mercy and grace. It is amazing to think that by merely presenting our bodies to God as a living and holy sacrifice, we are "acceptable to God" (Rom. 12:1-2).

The secret to holy living is not perfection but the total commitment of our whole self to serve God. We must live according to biblical standards of behavior, rather than conform to the standards and lifestyle of the world. As our lifestyle is transformed into conformity with the mind of Christ, we will become living examples of God's will—"good and acceptable and perfect." Patterns of holy living will be evidence of such a transformed heart and mind.

Discipline All Areas of Your Life

Patterns of holy living do not come without hard work and discipline. Peter states, "His divine power has given us everything we need for life and godliness." His gift does not, however, deny human responsibility. Throughout 2 Peter 1:2-11, Peter exhorts believers to "make every effort" to develop godly character. The passage as a whole indicates that if we have truly become partakers of the divine nature of God, we will strive to grow in holiness.

Paul also exhorts believers to discipline themselves for the purpose of godliness (1 Tim. 4:7-8). Discipline involves hard work. It is not always enjoyable, and seldom is it easy. Yet discipline is absolutely necessary in order to establish patterns of holy living (Heb. 12:1-11).

To grow spiritually, we must be disciplined in every area of life: social, mental, emotional, physical, and moral. Concerning our social life, we need to carefully evaluate the type of people we allow to influence us. We also need to set goals for ourselves concerning our intellectual development. This could mean setting up a regular pattern of stimulating reading, enrolling in a continuing education class, or attending a seminar or workshop. We must guard our emotional life so that neither past hurts nor present pressures monopolize our time or energy. Find healthy ways to express emotions through wholesome friendships, recreation, and hobbies. Keeping in shape physically, with a regular exercise program and a healthy diet, has a tremendous effect on both emotional and spiritual health.

Finally, the growing Christian needs to maintain strict discipline in the moral and ethical areas of life. Sexuality, power, and money all pose serious moral temptations to Christians in ministry, and in these areas one must be disciplined according to God's Word. Socially, mentally, emotionally, physically, and morally, we must maintain strict discipline in order to maintain a godly lifestyle.

The most important discipline in our life must be the daily practice of studying God's Word and talking to Him in prayer. One of the greatest spiritual dangers for the Christian worker is to become so preoccupied with outward ministry-related activities that the heart grows cold toward God. The result is often a shallow, busy ministry with little evidence of godliness. In addition to personal reflection, regular fellowship and worship with a body of believers are other mandatory disciplines for our growth in holy living. These disciplines must be established in our lives as a basis for ministry to others.

Be Accountable to Godly Christians

Active Christians tend to be lone rangers. They get going so fast and in so many directions that they fail to nurture quality relationships with other godly Christians who can hold them accountable. Busy Christians may sweep problems, habits, and sins under the carpet without properly dealing with them. They may ignore certain character weaknesses, hoping that God will magically overlook them. By the time some of these individuals seek help, it is too late. Their ministries, families, and relationships may have been severely damaged.

As disciples of Jesus, we all must be accountable on a deep interpersonal level to at least one other godly Christian outside our immediate family. These individuals should be people with whom they can confess even the most personal sins and faults (Jas. 5:16) and who are able to encourage them in holy living and stick with them in their "struggle against sin" (Heb. 12:4).

SUMMARY

Our effectiveness in ministry depends on our ability to maintain a godly lifestyle. Godliness reproduces itself. In order to establish such a lifestyle, we must cultivate a heart for God by opening ourselves up, confessing known sin, and allowing God to fill us with the power of the Holy Spirit. Second, we must learn to overcome temptation by admitting weaknesses, using God's resources, and guarding our thought life. Third, we must establish patterns of holy living by maintaining biblical standards in our lifestyle, disciplining all areas of our life, and being accountable to other godly Christians.

FOR FURTHER DISCUSSION

1. What are the three steps to establishing a godly lifestyle?
2. Why is it important that you open your heart to God?
3. What is the importance of daily confession of sin?
4. What part does the Holy Spirit play in establishing a godly lifestyle?
5. What are the three ways by which you can overcome temptation?
6. Give several biblical examples of people who were given God's strength in moments of their own physical weakness.
7. Why is the guarding of your thought life important?
8. Why are biblical standards still *the* standards to live by?
9. What importance does discipline play in establishing patterns of holy living?
10. Why is it important to be accountable to other Christians?

II.

EXPRESSIONS OF
SPIRITUAL GROWTH

Fruitfulness and Reaching Others for Christ

CHRIST'S STRATEGY FOR making disciples of all nations involves the church, as a body of believers, infiltrating every corner of the world with the love of Christ. The call to be loving witnesses to an unbelieving world should be the passion of every true follower of Christ. What does it mean to be a witness? A witness, in New Testament use, is simply a person who shares what he has experienced. A poignant example is found in John 9, where Jesus heals a man blind from birth. Jesus leaves the scene before the blind man can thank him. The blind man is surrounded by Pharisees who encourage him to denounce Jesus. They even go so far as to involve his parents, threatening to kick them out of the synagogue if they acknowledge Jesus as the Messiah. What is the blind man's response? "Whether he is a sinner or not, I don't know. One thing I do know. I was blind but now I see!" (John 9:25). The blind man was simply sharing what he had experienced. That is what it means to be a witness.

Jesus has chosen all believers to bear lasting fruit through their lives and ministry in the world (John 15:16-17). Yet this outward expression of our faith is only as good as our intimacy and obedience to Jesus Christ.

THE RESPONSIBILITY OF EVERY BELIEVER

Just as every believer is called into a relationship with Jesus Christ (Rom. 1:6; 1 Cor. 1:8), so every believer is called to express the love of Christ to others. There are many ways to show Christ's love. Paul affirms this point in Ephesians 4:12 when he states that the job of church leaders is to prepare all God's people to minister to, or serve, other people. One of the responsibilities of every Christian is to share the experience of his or her faith in Jesus Christ with others.

For this reason, we need to be careful not to focus on how much fruit we are producing. It would be a wiser investment of our energy to focus on deepening our relationship with Christ and to leave the results up to God. When it seems as if God is finished with us (during times of pruning), God could be preparing us for an even greater harvest. The fruit that comes from the life of a disciple of Jesus reflects the character, love, and productivity of Jesus Christ (Matt 7:17-20).

The Love of Christ

Love is the highest reflection of the character of God. Paul puts love at the top of his list of the fruit of the Spirit in Galatians 5:22-23: "The fruit of the Spirit is love, joy, peace, patience, kindness, goodness, faithfulness, gentleness and self-control." Again in 1 Corinthians 12—14, Paul emphasizes that love is the greatest of all of the fruit of the Holy Spirit. Love is the very core of all ministry gifts and abilities.

Jesus states that the way the world will know His disciples is by their love (John 13:35). Jesus puts love as the supreme test of discipleship (Matt. 25:31-46). Since God is love, and God expressed His love through Christ in us, it seems logical to assume that people who follow Jesus will be known for their love (1 John 4:7-21).

THE CALL TO ALL BELIEVERS

As we will discuss more fully in the next chapter, spiritual gifts provide the distinctive focus of each believer's ministry. For example, while some believers will focus on teaching, others will emphasize evangelism or hospitality. All believers are called to help a needy world with a loving witness. It is also true that some believers have been given the gift of evangelism, but all believers are to be like salt and light to a decaying and dark world (Matt. 5:13-16). The church's witness in the world will only be as strong as its ability to infiltrate the world with the love and message of Christ.

Where to Start

The apostolic pattern for reaching others is seen in Acts 1:8 when the Lord said, "You will be my witnesses in Jerusalem, and in all Judea and Samaria, and to the ends of the earth." This pattern is likened to ever-increasing circles when you drop a pebble in a pool. The beginning point is always the area closest to the point of impact. That usually means family, friends, and those one sees on a regular basis.

Developing Relationships Within the Family

The family is the laboratory where we learn to relate to others. The interpersonal skills and behaviors learned in the home are carried over into other areas of a person's life, the church, and the world. The Christian's first priority is a loving witness at home.

Husbands and Wives

Married believers must work diligently to develop submissive and loving relationships with their spouses. Such relationships model the organic relationship between Jesus Christ and His church. Couples need to plan mutually enjoyable activities with each other—regular Friday night dates, occasional mini-vacations for two, quiet evenings at home, regular times of prayer, and occasional rendezvous for lunch. Special times like these are essential in building warmth and trust.

Parents and Children

Many Christians are tempted to get so involved in ministry that they neglect their family. Children and parents alike need to be challenged to be more sensitive to each other's needs. Relationships take time to build. Children need to have plenty of time to spend with their parents if they are to assimilate the biblical values the parents hold. The quality of the parent-child relationship often determines whether or not the child follows the parents' biblical values.

LABORERS IN THE HARVEST

When the Acts 1:8 strategy is accepted as a biblical pattern for outreach, many priorities immediately become clearer. For example, home missions becomes the beginning point of ministry, and then it branches out to foreign missions. Today this pattern often becomes distorted, and evangelism efforts get reversed.

Jesus' ministry in the world was so radical that the Pharisees criticized Him for befriending tax-gatherers and sinners (Luke 7:34). In fact, Jesus Himself said that His mission was not to the so-called "righteous" but to the sinners (Matt. 9:13). Jesus spent a great deal of His time building relationships with people who were considered the worst of sinners. Yet He was able to avoid being affected by their ungodly values.

We need to guard against spending so much time on committees, projects, programs, and meetings with church people that we have no time or energy left to develop close relationships with non-Christians. We must maintain a balance in our personal relationships between Christians and non-Christians.

Robert Coleman, in *The Great Commission Life-style*, writes:

> Many churchmen have such an all-inclusive view of discipleship that the specific work of rescuing perishing souls from hell scarcely receives attention. Seeking to avoid this confusion of priorities . . . when I wrote my book on principles of discipling in the life of Christ, it was entitled *The Master Plan of Evangelism*. I wanted to emphasize that evangelism is the cutting edge of the Great Commission and that invariably it will flow out of a Christian life-style.[1]

Friendship Evangelism

God uses many evangelistic approaches to draw people into His kingdom. Friendship evangelism is an approach based simply on building relationships with non-Christians in normal daily contacts. Christians applying this method look for opportunities to demonstrate love and share their faith.

As growing and maturing Christians, we must be able to ask appropriate questions, listen, empathize, and tactfully bring in the gospel message at the right time. We must be able to maintain friendships with non-Christians in spite of their apparent apathy toward spiritual things.

James 4:4 warns Christians that "friendship with the world is hatred toward God." Here James makes a distinction between friendship with worldly people and friendship with worldly values. We are commanded to develop loving relationships with people in the world, but we must not be seduced by their worldly values. We must keep our distinction as salt and light in a needy world.

As even a single candle can illumine a dark pathway, so the light of the gospel bathes a lost world with the hope of Christ. The book of Romans contains the basics of this gospel message.

There are a multitude of evangelistic systems, formulas, or laws available to believers. A simple and yet tremendously powerful tool, often called the "Romans Road," is found in the book of Romans. Each of the verses is sequential and beautifully designed to help believers present Christ's plan of salvation to unbelievers.

The Romans Road begins with Romans 3:10 and its declaration that "there is no one righteous, not even one." Supporting this first step is 3:23: "For all have sinned and fall short of the glory of God." This first step strips unbelievers of any self-righteousness before God.

A second step is the need to identify unbelievers with Adam's sin found in 5:17: "For if, by the trespass of the one man, death reigned through that one man, how much more will those who receive God's abundant provision of grace and of the gift of righteousness reign in life through the one man, Jesus Christ." This confirms that everyone has inherited Adam's sinful nature.

In 6:23 unbelievers are challenged with the gift that is theirs if they accept it by faith: "For the wages of sin is death, but the gift of God is eternal life in Christ Jesus our Lord." This is the third step.

From that passage, the evangelist can take unbelievers to 10:9-10, the fourth step, which reads, "That if you confess with your mouth, 'Jesus is Lord,' and believe in your heart that God raised him from the dead, you will be saved. For it is with your heart that you believe and are justified, and it is with your mouth that you confess and are saved."

Developing a Passion to Reach People in All Nations for Christ

The Great Commission ultimately calls the church to make disciples of all nations. While the Acts 1:8 strategy begins in Jerusalem, it ends up touching people at the far corners of the globe. Christ's desire was that all the great peoples of the world would come to know Him. The church will be fruitful in fulfilling its commission to the degree that it fulfills Christ's passion to see all the nations respond to the gospel. The church must continually set before its people the ultimate challenge of the Great Commission.

SUMMARY

The call of the church to make disciples of people from every nation means that every Christian must use his or her God-given gifts and abilities to be a witness to a needy world. Regardless of the diversity of special gifts within the body of Christ, all believers are called to be fruitful witnesses of Christ's love to others. Our witness begins with those we are the closest to, like family and friends. It then extends to our community and eventually to the far ends of the earth. Fruitfulness in ministry depends on God and our connection to Jesus Christ through the Holy Spirit. For this reason intimacy with Christ is the key to our witness to other people. The ultimate challenge for the church today is to renew its commitment to share Christ's love with people in various parts of the globe who as yet have not heard the Good News.

FOR FURTHER DISCUSSION

1. In what way is the gift of evangelism different from the responsibility that all believers have to reach out to the lost and needy around them?

2. Why do you think that Jesus gave His disciples the strategy to begin reaching out close to home, then to move farther away to the more remote areas?

3. Why is it so important for a person to establish a successful ministry in his or her family before investing a lot of time in ministry with people outside it?

8

Discovering and Using Our Spiritual Gifts

ONE OF THE FIRST lessons we must learn as growing Christians is that we are saved to serve. In contrast to the popular values in today's me-centered culture, we are not saved merely to satisfy ourselves. We are saved by a sovereign Lord to fulfill His plan for the world. We have not been simply given a fire escape from hell. We have received the unique privilege of serving the most High God. And what a tremendous privilege that is!

Our sovereign God needs absolutely nothing in order to complete His plan for this world. The same Lord who spoke the world into existence needs no mere human instrument to assist Him in the magnificent task of sustaining it. Yet He has chosen human beings to do just that. As Jesus said, "You did not choose me, but I chose you and appointed you to go and bear fruit—fruit that will last" (John 15:16).

Along with the general commission given to all believers to make disciples and to be loving witnesses of Christ, the Lord has given specific ministry gifts to each believer. It is important to note that both the task of making disciples and the gifts to accomplish that task are given to the body of believers as a whole. A dangerous tendency, especially in our individualistic culture, may be to try to focus too much on developing and using our gifts rather than contributing to the unified ministry of the body of Christ.

WHERE DO THE MINISTRY GIFTS COME FROM?

Christ gave spiritual gifts to the church when He made His triumphal ascension into heaven after His victory over Satan on the cross. The analogy that Paul uses to describe this event comes from an ancient military practice. When a victorious army returned from winning a battle, they would parade their captives in chains through the city and give the residents of the city gifts taken from the conquered land. With this background the following Scripture makes a lot more sense: "But to each one of us grace has been given as Christ apportioned it. This is why it says: 'When he ascended on high, he led captives in his train and gave gifts to men'" (Eph. 4:7-8). Spiritual gifts are given by God because of His grace toward His people. In Scripture all three persons of the Trinity—the Father, the Son, and the Holy Spirit—are mentioned as the givers of spiritual gifts (1 Cor. 12:4-6). Gifts began to be exercised by the church when the Holy Spirit was given on the Day of Pentecost. That is why they are referred to as the gifts of the Spirit.

WHO RECEIVES MINISTRY GIFTS?

God sovereignly gives specific gifts to individuals and arranges them within the body of Christ to accomplish His purposes (1 Cor. 12:18). Since they are gifts of God's grace, we can take no credit for them. Yet each and every believer in the body of Christ is given a gift (Eph. 4:7). Not to acknowledge a gift from God Almighty is not a sign of humility but rather of ingratitude. For this reason we need to be careful that we don't downplay God's gifts of grace in our lives.

A common misinterpretation of Scripture has led to a major misunderstanding of the term *ministry* in the church today. The concept that the pastor is the only real minister has often squelched the layperson's passion for ministry. Yet Scripture teaches that one of the main roles of the pastor/teacher is "to prepare God's people for works of service" (Eph. 4:12). The word for "service" could also be translated as "ministry." The source of the erroneous understanding of the term *ministry* came from verse 12 of Ephesians 4. The early King James Version of the Bible translated the text as if the role of the pastor/teacher were threefold: "for the perfecting of the saints, for the work of the ministry, for the edifying of the body of Christ." Thus it could easily be inferred that the pastor's responsibility involved three distinct things: to perfect the saints, to do the work of the ministry, and to edify the church. This interpretation is radically different from the original intent of the text. In the Greek, the three phrases connect directly to one another. A much more accurate translation of the text would read: "It was he who gave some to be apostles, some to be prophets, some to be evangelists, and some to be pastors and teachers, to prepare God's people for works of service, so that the body of Christ may be built up" (Eph. 4:11-12). Pastors are not the only ones who do the work of the ministry; rather their job is to prepare God's people to minister. The real ministers are the people in the pews. The church leaders minister by training and preparing the other ministers to use their spiritual gifts to serve others (1 Pet. 4:10), so that the body of Christ is built up and grows toward "the whole measure of the fullness of Christ" (Eph. 4:13).

WHY ARE THE MINISTRY GIFTS GIVEN?

Ministry gifts are given to believers in the body to enable them to minister to others and to build up the body of Christ (Eph. 4:12-13; 1 Cor. 12:7). As a result of Christians serving each other sacrificially according to their giftedness, the body grows stronger, becomes more unified, and becomes more mature (Eph. 4:13). Spiritual gifts were not given to elevate certain individuals within a local body. These supernatural manifestations of the Holy Spirit were given to the church and its members to empower them to fulfill the Great Commission. The gifts of the Spirit were at least part of what Jesus had in mind when He told His disciples that when the Holy Spirit came, they would do even greater works of ministry (John 14:12). The supernatural gifts of the Holy Spirit were given to build up the universal church as well as local churches for the accomplishment of their mission.

WHAT ARE THE DIFFERENT TYPES OF GIFTS?

In order to accomplish the task of world discipleship, God empowered the church through a variety of different spiritual gifts. These varied gifts accommodate people's different needs, passions, personalities, and learning styles. Although extensive lists of different spiritual gifts can be found in 1 Corinthians 12, Romans 12, Ephesians 4, and 1 Peter 4, even these lists are not necessarily exhaustive. The lists of spiritual gifts included in the New Testament adequately explain how God gifted the early church to minister. There are many reasons to suggest that God is not limited to only these gifts today. God gives gifts in every culture to supernaturally empower His people to minister effectively in that culture. It is important not to limit God's ability to give people supernatural gifts and abilities to minister in new ways within a rapidly changing world.

The gifts listed in the New Testament may be categorized under speaking, serving, and signifying gifts.

Speaking Gifts

1. Apostleship (Eph. 4:11)—the present-day missionary or church-planting gift.
2. Prophecy (Eph. 4:11)—foretelling and/or proclaiming (forthtelling) in a demonstrative way the truth of God.
3. Evangelism (Eph. 4:11)—special abilities in communicating the gospel to unbelievers.
4. Teaching (Eph. 4:11)—a unique ability to help people to learn and obey the Word of God.
5. Exhortation (Rom. 12:8)—counseling, encouraging, and challenging others.
6. Knowledge and wisdom (1 Cor. 12:8)—the ability to gain deep insight into the Word of God and share its application to the problems of life.

Serving Gifts

1. Helps (1 Cor. 12:28)—the ability to serve others in a supportive role.
2. Hospitality (1 Pet. 4:9; Rom. 12:13)—the special ability to provide an open house and warm welcome for those in need of food, lodging, or companionship.
3. Giving (Rom. 12:8)—more than tithing, this is the gift of generosity toward the cause of Christ.
4. Administration (1 Cor. 12:28)—the special gift of leadership and administration.
5. Mercy (Rom. 12:8)—a gift of empathy and compassion toward those who are needy.
6. Faith (1 Cor. 12:9)—the ability to envision what God wants done and persevere through obstacles to completion.
7. Discernment (1 Cor. 12:10)—a special ability to distinguish between the Spirit of truth and the spirit of error.

Signifying Gifts

1. Miracles (1 Cor. 12:10)—the ability to draw on God's supernatural power to accomplish God's purposes.
2. Healing (1 Cor. 12:9)—a supernatural ability to be instrumental in curing illness and restoring health.
3. Tongues (1 Cor. 12:28)—Three positions are debated: (a) emit-

ting ecstatic utterances, (b) using a previously unknown language, or (c) both. Some believe interpretation is included with this gift. Others believe the interpretation of tongues is a separate gift.

Although some theologians disagree as to whether or not all of the signifying gifts are applicable today, we must be careful never to limit God by our own theological systems.

How Do We Find Out Which Gifts We Have?

Unfortunately when God adopted us into His family, He did not give us our birthday gift wrapped up in a fancy package. He realized that in the process of discovery we tend to appreciate the things we learn much more.

To discover our spiritual gifts we must do four things: identify our strengths and weaknesses, evaluate our spiritual passion, get feedback from Christian friends, and use the process of trial and error to identify the area of our giftedness.

Identify Our Strengths and Weaknesses

The first step in determining our spiritual gifts is to identify our strengths and weaknesses. God can certainly give people spiritual gifts outside their natural abilities, but our natural affinities are a good place to start. The question we need to ask ourselves is, "What things that I do for others has God blessed and used in building up other people and the ministry of the church?" On the other hand, "What sorts of things have I done that have been frustrating or counterproductive in ministering to others?" As we uncover these successes and failures, evidences of effectiveness and ineffectiveness, or strengths and weaknesses in our ministry attempts, a pattern will emerge that will reveal those gifts that God has given us.

Evaluate Our Spiritual Passions

When we sense the spark of passion for a particular ministry, it indicates at least a leaning toward a particular spiritual gift. Too often Christians downplay passion in the Christian life. Strong emotional feelings are a valuable part of a Christian's experience (Ps. 37:4).

Get Feedback from Christian Friends

Since spiritual gifts are given to the body of Christ as a whole, it is important to look to the people we are close to for feedback related to what we perceive our gifts to be. Sunday school teachers, mentors, elders, family members, pastors, and close friends can give us valuable feedback.

Use the Process of Trial and Error

We have all heard the expression, "We learn by doing." This principle is even truer in the process of discovering our spiritual gifts. People often are not even aware of their gifts until they get out and do ministry. For this reason it is a good practice in the church to allow people the opportunity to serve in different types of ministries. It is also a good practice to allow people to fail gracefully as they test out their gifts and abilities. Sometimes the best lessons in ministry come from failure rather than success.

In addition to these four principles on how to discover our spiritual gifts, there are many well-developed inventories to help us discern what our gifts, passions, and ministry interests are.

SUMMARY

Identifying our ministry gifts is an important part of our continued maturing in Christ. By using our Spirit-given gifts to minister to others, we contribute to the building of the body of Christ, and we glorify God. The wide variety of gifts identified in the Bible are an indication of the diversity of people's needs and temperaments. A thoughtful examination of our life and consultation with other believers within the context of the church will help us to discover our ministry gifts. After identifying these gifts, we need to develop and use them faithfully in serving the Lord.

FOR FURTHER DISCUSSION

1. What is the difference between ministry gifts and talents?
2. What guidelines should you follow in determining your gifts?
3. What are some ways in which you can develop your gifts?
4. What other gifts do you think God might add to the biblical lists if He were writing to us in this culture?
5. Why must we be careful not to focus too much on our individual gifts?

9

Teaching Others

ONE OF THE BEST ways to learn something is to learn it well enough to teach it to someone else. Skiing in Canada when I was growing up gave me a head start over other college students when it came to winter sports. I was asked to teach skiing classes my freshman year. I thought I was pretty good at slushing down the hills myself, but it was a different story when it came to teaching a bunch of scared neophytes to do it. I discovered that the best way to learn the fundamentals of skiing is to teach others.

This principle is even truer when teaching other people how to know and apply God's Word. In fact, for those who truly have the gift of teaching, the process of teaching itself actually energizes them to get closer to God and to dig more into His Word.

WHAT IS THE GIFT OF TEACHING?

The gift of teaching is the supernatural ability to communicate God's Word in a way that motivates people to understand it within the context of their lives and obey its principles. The goal for teaching comes directly from the Great Commission where teaching is listed as one of the three ways we are to fulfill the command to make disciples: "*teaching* them to obey everything I have commanded you" (Matt. 28:20, italics added). In this verse two phrases give insight into what Jesus meant. The first phrase, "teaching them to obey," gives us the main focus of our teaching. The direct object of "teaching" is not the "Word" but rather "to obey." Teaching people to obey God's Word is much more complex than teaching mere content. Jesus was never satisfied with teaching for the transmission of knowledge with no effect on behavior. Truly knowing God and His Word affects a person's whole life.

The second phrase in this text, "everything I have commanded you," answers the question about "what" the learners are to obey. Yet to put these two phrases out of order is to miss the whole point of what it means to make disciples of Jesus Christ. Certainly God's Word is important to Jesus. In fact, Jesus, by both His use of Scripture and His teaching about Scripture, shows that He was a diligent student of the Word. Jesus never taught that the study of Scripture was an end in itself. In fact, He condemned the religious leaders for believing that salvation came through the actual study of Scripture (John 5:39-40). His disciples not only know His Word, but they obey it (Matt. 7:24; Luke 11:28).

"Whoever practices and teaches these commands will be called great in the kingdom of heaven" (Matt. 5:19). Practicing the truth is a prerequisite for teaching the truth. Obedience is learned by imitation, not legislation.

DIFFERENT TYPES OF TEACHING

Good teachers come in all shapes and sizes: single parents who faithfully bring up their children to obey the Word, boys' club leaders who maintain a relationship with their guys long into their adult years, Sunday school teachers who take the time to do fun activities with their students, Bible study group leaders who skillfully build a sense of community with their members, or a men's or women's group leader who faithfully helps group members get victory over addictive behaviors.

In Deuteronomy 6:5-9, we discover three types of teaching commonly found in the home: modeling, formal, and informal teaching. A fourth type is nonformal teaching (often used by Jesus).

Modeling

If we expect others to adopt biblical values, we must be passionate about what we teach. Moses was keenly aware of this principle when he began his instruction to the Hebrew parents with the challenge recorded in Deuteronomy 6:5-6. One of the best ways to affect the behavior of others is to passionately live the values you want to teach in front of your students.

Formal

When Moses tells parents to "impress" God's commandments upon their children (Deut 6:7), he wants them to reinforce the laws of God continually in the hearts and minds of their children. This process would imply a more formal teaching strategy in the home that would systematically and intentionally help children to learn the laws of God. Adults plan how to use the teaching opportunities that they have each day in the home, school, or church.

Informal

The third type of teaching alluded to in the Deuteronomy text relates to what educators call informal teaching. As the text illustrates (vv. 7-9), informal teaching is instruction that is initiated by the circumstances and situations of an informal setting. It is unplanned and part of the natural environment. Educators often explain informal teaching as taking advantage of the teachable moments that arise in everyday life. In a Christian context this implies looking for opportunities to engage the learner in reflecting, questioning, and discussing issues. It concerns helping the student discover or reinforce biblical principles.

Nonformal

Although not cited in the above passage, another important type of teaching was used by Jesus—nonformal teaching. This process is similar to informal in that it happens within the informal living environment. It is different from informal in that it is planned and intentional. Because it combines the strengths of these two types of teaching, it can be an effective way to intentionally accomplish specific goals within an informal context. It allows for more student participation and interaction with more opportunity for application as well. Gifted teachers offer a variety of approaches to meet students' needs. A church or other institution is wise to develop people at their different levels of Christian maturity.

LEARNING FROM JESUS THE TEACHER

In the Gospels, Jesus is referred to as a teacher more than by any other title. The Greek word most often given to Christ, as an educational title, is *didaskalos*. This word is translated "teacher" or "master" and is found more than forty times in the Gospels. Most frequently in the King James Version of the Bible, *didaskalos* is translated "master" rather than "teacher" because at the time of translation the word *master* was understood to mean "schoolmaster."

- Jesus' disciples referred to Him as teacher or master (Mark 4:38).
- The scribes and Pharisees referred to Him in this way (John 3:2).
- Jesus identified Himself by the term (Mark 14:14).

Other Bible passages also point out the priority of teaching in the ministry of Christ (Matt. 4:23; 5:2; 7:29).

Rabbi is another title associated with the word *teacher* and is used to refer to Christ. This word is also sometimes translated "master" and, as a Jewish title, designated one as able to teach with the authority of Moses, possessing authority to interpret the law. Nicodemus and the disciples of John the Baptist called Jesus "Rabbi" (John 1:38; 3:2). *Rabboni* (John 20:16), a similar but even more intensively educational and relational title, was used by Mary Magdalene when He appeared to her after the Resurrection.

Christ taught in a variety of situations: *one-on-one* teaching (personal interaction, John 4:1-42); *small group* learning (the disciples alone with Christ, Luke 22:14-38); *large groups* of people (the multitudes heard Him, Matt. 23:1-39). Believers today are responsible to continue the Lord's teaching ministry in all situations.

PRINCIPLES OF EFFECTIVE TEACHING

Principles of effective teaching must be based on what actually helps people to grow and develop into maturity in Jesus Christ. The source for these principles must be God's Word. Many of the following principles are based upon what we have already discussed in chapter 1.

Effective teaching helps people to grow more like Christ and focuses on these six principles:

1. Knowing God
2. Knowing God's Word
3. Knowing How People Learn
4. Applying Truth to the Whole Person
5. Helping People to Obey the Word
6. Balancing Support and Challenge

Knowing God

For a teacher to teach and students to learn, each must be properly connected to the Vine, Jesus Christ. Obviously a teacher must model such a connection to motivate others to follow. The teacher, however, must also challenge and train students in how to develop their own relationships with Christ. The optimal learning environment is one in which both the students and the teacher are passionately seeking to know and follow Christ. Everything possible must encourage this team effort.

Knowing God's Word

Regardless of the teaching style used, the focus of a learning experience must be God's Word. The teacher must set the example by maintaining a regular habit of studying God's Word daily. In this way a teacher will be spiritually prepared to utilize teaching opportunities ranging from the brief teachable moments of informal settings to impromptu questions in a formal classroom.

Knowing How People Learn

It does not matter how entertaining a teacher is. If students do not learn, the experience is of little value within the kingdom of God. Teachers must take the time to get to know their students personally to identify how they learn best. Teaching methods are then carefully chosen with the developmental needs of students and educational goals in mind.

Applying Truth to the Whole Person

Spiritual growth and development applies to every aspect of people's lives. A good church or Christian education program should balance goals and plan for needs including the physical, social, emotional, moral, and intellectual areas. Spiritual goals need to be integrated into each of these areas of growth to help students apply God's truth to the whole person.

Helping People to Obey the Word

The task of the Christian teacher would be fairly simple if our goal was simply to help people understand God's Word. Our commission, however, goes far beyond acquiring knowledge and changing immediate behavior. We must teach people to *obey* God's Word. This requires higher thinking skills, more time, more prayer, more spiritual energy, and a greater commitment to follow up from the teacher. It demands that the teacher be aware of how the students apply the principles learned.

Balancing Support and Challenge

When we look at the seemingly impossible challenges of the cost of discipleship in Scripture, we realize that the only way we can even attempt to move toward the goal of Christlikeness is in response to Christ's love. He balanced His challenge with His support in giving us so many gifts of His grace: the presence of the Comforter, the Holy Spirit, the encouragement of the body of Christ, the gift of unconditional forgiveness, His precious promises, and the final promise to be with us always (Matt. 28:20). By focusing on these principles, effective teaching helps others to grow more like Christ.

SUMMARY

For the Christian, teaching is a unique privilege that may take different forms: formal, informal, nonformal, and modeling. The focus of Christian teaching should be changed lives. It takes all types of teachers to be instrumental in helping the variety of people in the body of Christ to grow.

Jesus is one of the best examples of a teacher in all of history. When we follow Christ, our example as the Teacher, we will not only challenge our students to Christlikeness but also show them warmth and grace when they fall short.

FOR FURTHER DISCUSSION

1. How can teaching God's Word help us grow spiritually?
2. What are some of the signs that a person has the gift of teaching?
3. Name some ways that all believers are teachers as they live and witness in the world.
4. How did Jesus stand out as a teacher?
5. Under what styles of teaching do you learn best?

10

Leading Others

ALL CHRISTIANS WHO are truly growing spiritually will be involved in some form of leadership. Given the vast array of needs in the world today, each Christian should be able to find a satisfying leadership role in the home, church, or society. The Scriptures require leadership responsibility in all areas of life.

God has given specialized leadership gifts within the church to provide vision and direction. In Ephesians 4:11, Paul gives us a list of leadership positions based on specific gifts related to apostleship, prophecy, evangelism, pastoring, and teaching. These positions may seem more prominent within the church, but they should never overshadow the gifts of leadership given to other lay ministers within the body of Christ. A key growth factor for the church rests in all members taking leadership to use their gifts in service to others (Eph. 4:16).

Society needs to see the moral and ethical influences of Christian leadership. Government, education, media, entertainment, science, health, and social services all need to be infiltrated by loving, godly Christians. Yet leadership in society must be administered through the believer's life and witness. Even the earliest society of Adam and Eve was charged with having dominion (or authority) over the creation (Gen. 1:26). Psalm 8 also states that God gave man leadership responsibility over all of creation (v. 6). In addition, Jesus described the leadership role of believers as being "the salt of the earth" and "the light of the world" so that others might see their good works and glorify God (Matt. 5:13-16). Mature Christians have a God-given responsibility to serve Him as leaders within God's creation and society.

Leadership is required of every believer, not just a few select individuals. We may not all have official positions of leadership, but we do all have the responsibility to lead others in some area of our giftedness.

Leadership, from a Christian perspective, is a God-given ability to provide vision and direction to accomplish God's will within His kingdom. Leadership is using one's gifts and abilities in loving service to a person or group for the sake of Christ. The result of biblical leadership is the growth of individuals and groups in Christlikeness.

PRINCIPLES OF CHRISTIAN LEADERSHIP

Jesus established radical standards related to how we should love others and instituted radical principles as to how we should lead others. These principles become more distinctive when we realize how authoritarian the leadership structure was in the Roman and Jewish culture of Jesus' day. The three principles undergirding Christian leadership are integrity in character, a servant's attitude, and an equipping vision.

Integrity in Character

Even contemporary secular authors reinforce a principle long held by Christians: Effective leadership is built upon a disciplined inner life and a strong character. The word *integrity* describes a person whose thoughts and private behavior are consistent with their outward profession. The Christian leader with integrity is a person whose heart is set on loving and obeying God, no matter what the cost.

Daniel powerfully illustrates this principle for us in his rise to leadership in the Babylonian empire. He maintained his regular practice of praying to God even though it meant getting thrown to the lions (Dan. 6). The New Testament also emphasizes this principle. The majority of qualifications for church leaders mentioned by Paul relate to character rather than skills (1 Tim. 3:1-10; Tit. 1:7-9). Our tendency may be to take shortcuts to get to where we want to go in our ministry career, but integrity demands that Christian leaders invest the necessary time and energy to build spiritual consistency in the soul. Only then will God bless us in our outward ministry.

A Servant's Attitude

This characteristic is often associated with the ministry of Christ. Our Lord is seen in Scripture as a servant. One of the best-known passages on servant-leadership occurs when the mother of James and John asks Jesus about leadership roles and positions for her two sons. Jesus' reply was:

> *You know that the rulers of the Gentiles lord it over them, and their*
> *high officials exercise authority over them. Not so with you. Instead,*
> *whoever wants to become great among you must be your servant, and*
> *whoever wants to be first must be your slave—just as the Son of Man*
> *did not come to be served, but to serve, and to give his life a ransom for*
> *many. (Matt. 20:25-28)*

On another occasion Christ said, "The greatest among you will be your servant" (Matt. 23:11).

Two of the many examples of servanthood that Christ demonstrated were in situations where He cared for His disciples in very practical ways. Before the Last Supper, Jesus washed the disciples' feet (John 13:1-11). After His resurrection, He prepared breakfast for them on the beach (John 21:9-14). If we are to follow Christ as a leader, we must follow His example and serve those we lead. There is a dangerous tendency, as churches and Christian organizations get bigger and more powerful, for leaders to move away from this basic principle of Christian leadership.

Yet we must be careful not to call *servanthood* a style of leadership. It really has nothing to do with style. It is primarily an attitude of the heart that may express itself in various styles depending on the circumstances and needs. A Christian leader with a servant's heart may find it appropriate to use an assertive approach to get something done and on another occasion respond more meekly. Regardless of the style of leadership used in a certain situation, the Christian leader must be motivated by a heart to serve God and others.

An Equipping Vision

One of the major roles of church leaders is to prepare, train, or equip Christians in the church to use their gifts to minister to one another in the body. Church leaders are the spark that ignites the fire that spreads between members to help each other grow and mature into the likeness of Christ. "It was he who gave some to be . . . pastors and teachers, to prepare God's people for works of service, so that the body of Christ may be built up until we all reach unity in the faith and in the knowledge of the Son of God and become mature, attaining to the whole measure of the fullness of Christ" (Eph. 4:11-13).

If church leaders are to be successful in helping the body of Christ to mature, they must have a vision to invest in preparing others to utilize their gifts to minister within the body. Once again this vision is very different from what normally drives people into positions of leadership. It takes humility and a servant's heart to use one's gifts to empower other believers for ministry, rather than focusing on establishing one's own position or career. When a leader's power is shared, it multiplies; when it is used to further one's own ends, it corrupts.

These three principles—integrity of character, a servant's attitude, and a vision to equip others—must be in the heart of a leader interested in helping others to grow and mature in Christ. In addition there are five skills that leaders must learn in order to be effective in leading others.

LEADERSHIP SKILLS

Vision Building

All the great leaders mentioned in Scripture had a vision: Noah—to save his people from the flood; Abraham—to settle the Promised Land; Moses—to set his people free; Joshua—to recapture the Promised Land; Solomon—to build a great temple for God; Jeremiah—to rebuild the walls of Jerusalem; and Paul—to see Gentiles come to the Lord. Leaders initiate and carry out a vision.

Visions that further the kingdom of God, however, must be in accordance with God's will. Most of us can give illustrations of idealistic people who dreamed up a lofty vision and got others to follow them. Then when the leader left, the vision died. Visions from God are based upon solid biblical principles and are verified by the body of Christ. The best protection against a leader going off on an egotistical crusade is to build a vision together with other members in the body of Christ. The one advantage we have over the people in the Old Testament is the presence of Christ in the corporate gathering of the church. Too often we do not take advantage of the energy and wisdom that comes from other believers who are following Christ closely. If we want to develop leadership within the body of Christ, then we should share the vision-building process with them. When people have been a part of the planning, they are more apt to take the responsibility to carry the plan through.

Empathetic Listening

The second skill of an effective leader is the ability to empathize with the thoughts, feelings, and frustrations of other people. Since many "natural" leaders tend to be more direct and goal-centered, this skill is one that will have to be intentionally developed. People tend to follow leaders who have a clear idea of where they are going and who are also sensitive to the concerns of those around them.

In Philippians 2:3-4 we are challenged, "Do nothing out of selfish ambition or vain conceit, but in humility consider others better than yourselves. Each of you should look not only to your own interests, but also to the interests of others." Since this advice is given to all believers, we can be sure that it applies even more to those of us desiring to be leaders.

Practically, this means spending time with each of those we work with. It means asking good questions that help other people to express their inner thoughts and feelings. It means being more concerned about others' personal lives than their contribution to the "cause." People can pick up very quickly whether or not we are genuinely interested in them as individuals. Our goal needs to be to make every person on our team feel significant and special. While this will obviously take time and effort, the investment in others' lives will bring rich dividends of loyalty and commitment. People follow those who sincerely care for them.

Empowering Others

After leaders train and equip people in the church to use their ministry gifts, the next step is to empower them to minister or serve. The concept of empowering others implies that the leader shares power with another person. A good example of this is when a father confidently tells his daughter that she can mow the lawn by herself this time. The child is motivated by the confidence that the father places in her to accomplish a new task. Power is transferred from father to daughter. The same thing happens when a leader empowers another gifted person for a ministry. By giving away both the responsibility and the rewards of ministry, leaders allow their people to enjoy the rich benefits of serving others.

Empowering others for ministry is similar to the process of delegation except that delegation usually relates more directly to a task than a ministry. Delegating responsibility involves the use and transmission of authority. For delegation to occur, Christians need confidence and trust in one another. Yet to be effective, tasks should only be delegated to people with the gifts and abilities to accomplish them. For example, there would be no basis for appointing someone to be responsible for a youth group if he or she had no experience working with students or had little knowledge of Scripture.

One of the clearest biblical examples of delegation is seen in the advice given by Jethro to his son-in-law Moses. Jethro observed that Moses was overwhelmed, overextended, and overworked by spending all of his time singlehandedly judging the people (Exod. 18:13). In response to the situation, he advised Moses to delegate responsibility as explained in Exodus 18:17-22.

New Testament examples of delegation of responsibility in relation to Christ include John 5:27 and Matthew 28:18-21. In the John passage, the Father gives authority to the Son to accomplish His purposes. In the Matthew passage, Jesus gives responsibility to His disciples based upon His authority. "All authority in heaven and on earth has been given to me. Therefore go and make disciples of all nations." Empowering others for ministry is a leadership skill directly linked to the growth of the kingdom of God.

Team Building

The fourth skill necessary for effective leadership is the ability to inspire others to work together as a cohesive team. The church is not just a random group of individuals. Rather, it is an interconnected team of followers of Christ. Unity and love are values that are elevated in Scripture even above success and personal accomplishment (Eph. 4:1-6). Paul goes on in chapter 4 to explain that "speaking the truth in love, we will in all things grow up into him who is the Head, that is, Christ. From him the whole body, joined and held together by every supporting ligament, grows and builds itself up in love, as each part does its work" (vv. 15-16). A major leadership skill is helping the members of the body to work cooperatively while using their gifts and following their visions. Part of this skill is encouraging the "ligaments" to support one another in this process.

Conflict Resolution

The fifth skill for effective leadership is the ability to help people resolve conflicts. Where there are people, there are problems. This is as true for the church as it is for any other organization. Yet if conflicts are not dealt with in accordance with biblical principles, they can destroy people's lives and the unity within the body of Christ.

The skill of helping people resolve conflicts involves several aspects. Leaders must be courageous enough to deal with major conflicts rather than just ignoring them. Often there is a cost involved in dealing with conflict, particularly if the problem has been brooding for a long time and was ignored by previous leaders. Leaders must be objective enough to listen to the facts and feelings of all the parties involved. This process demands good "detective" skills. The leader needs to help the parties involved to listen to each other and try to empathize with the other party's feelings. In helping to reach a resolution to the conflict, the leader must demonstrate a thorough knowledge of God's Word and be able to clearly teach what the biblical alternatives to the conflict are. Finally the leader must be able to help the parties come to a mutually acceptable decision based upon scriptural principles.

As complex as this process sounds, it is one of the most important skills of a leader. As many of us can verify, one of the main reasons why people leave the church, full-time ministry, and missionary service is because of unresolved interpersonal conflicts.

SUMMARY

The home, the church, and society desperately need strong Christian leaders. Yet before volunteering too quickly, we must count the cost of following Christ as a leader. The radical standards of Christian leadership demand that leaders are men and women of integrity, with hearts to serve and a vision to prepare others to serve. These standards are quite different from the way the rest of the world looks at leadership. To be effective Christian leaders, we must continually develop our skills in these five areas: building a vision, empathetic listening, empowering others, team building, and conflict resolution. While the cost of leadership is high, the rewards are great. To see others in the body of Christ growing and using their gifts in ministry is one of the greatest blessings we will ever experience.

FOR FURTHER DISCUSSION

1. In what ways should a Christian leader be different from leaders of the world?
2. Why might empowering others be difficult for some leaders?
3. Identify and give an example of each of the leadership skills discussed in this chapter.
4. What biblical leaders stand out in your mind as good leaders? Why did you choose them?
5. Give an example of a situation in which a leader may have to be assertive in being a servant-leader.

11

Mentoring Others

MENTORING RELATIONSHIPS are one of the most significant ways Christians can help other Christians to grow spiritually. People have mentored one another since the beginning of time. Only the terminology has changed. The term *mentor* has become more popular today because of the increased need for one-on-one relationships to address contemporary culture's intimacy vacuum. The rise of technology and decline of the family structure have increased our need to bond through learning. Mentoring seems to provide the "high touch" in a "high tech" world.

WHAT IS MENTORING?

Mentoring is a relational process between an older, more mature, more knowledgeable, *or* more skilled person and another person who learns in some intentional way. Age cannot necessarily be equated with a higher level of maturity, knowledge, or skill. One of the primary components of mentoring is the relational process itself. For this reason some people may be more skilled at mentoring than others. Relational skill is needed to make a mentoring partnership work. What distinguishes a mentoring relationship from other informal learning is intentionality. In a mentoring relationship the mentoree establishes with the mentor specifically what he wants to learn, and together they establish how he will learn it. With the focus on learning rather than teaching, both persons in the relationship will have a deeper level of responsibility in the process.

PRINCIPLES OF MENTORING FROM SCRIPTURE

Mentoring has been used since early civilization to teach and train others for a variety of purposes. Throughout Scripture we find many illustrations of key biblical leaders being mentored. Mentoring is one of the primary ways God uses people to help others learn, grow, and develop as well as to mold them into the kind of people He wants them to be. We will examine three mentoring relationships from Scripture to identify principles we can use today.

Elijah and Elisha

Elijah and Elisha were two prophets who fought against the evil influences of Baalism in Israel's early history. Elijah prepared the way by confronting the wicked Queen Jezebel and by killing all the prophets of Baal on Mount Carmel. Even after that tremendous victory, he felt alone and depressed. In his despair, God spoke to him and gave him hope. Part of that hope was in choosing a successor and companion for Elijah in the person of Elisha. This new relationship began as a result of God choosing Elisha. In 1 Kings 19:19 we find that "Elijah went from there and found Elisha." Elisha then "set out to follow Elijah and became his attendant" (v. 21b). Elisha learned how to be a prophet of God by being with Elijah, watching him, and listening to him continually. We could refer to this as the first "prophet apprenticeship school." Apparently Elisha learned his lessons well. When Elijah was taken up to heaven in a chariot of God, Elisha immediately took up Elijah's cloak (the passing on of the baton), and all those watching realized that the "spirit of Elijah is resting on Elisha" (2 Kings 2:11-15). Elisha went on to do even greater things than Elijah in his ministry. What an example of a successful mentoring relationship! A major principle of mentoring is to train others to accomplish even greater things than we do.

Barnabas and Paul

This next example dramatically illustrates the principle that our goal is to empower others to use their gifts and ministries even to the point of seeing their ministry reach beyond our own.

If you will recall the early life of Saul after his conversion experience, he was blind and without a friend. Ananias was the first to welcome him into the church fellowship (Acts 9:17), but the Christians in Jerusalem were still too frightened to associate with him because of his past reputation. Barnabas was responsible for introducing Saul into the core group of church leaders (Acts 9:27-28).

Barnabas encouraged Paul to use his gifts of teaching and preaching wherever they traveled. When Luke records their travels together in the book of Acts, he begins by always mentioning them in the order of "Barnabas and Saul" (Acts 11:26; 13:2). Yet after their ministry in Cyprus, Luke changes the order throughout the rest of the book of Acts to "Paul and Barnabas" (Acts 13:13). The reason for the change in order is obvious after reading the account of what happened in Cyprus (Acts 13:4-12). God chose to bless Paul's ministry in such a mighty way that Paul apparently was looked upon as the leader of the duo from that point on.

What a lesson in humility for us in ministry today. Would we be willing to pour our lives into another person only to see their ministry overshadow ours? That is exactly the point of Barnabas' ministry. Perhaps in heaven his reward will be even greater than that of Paul because he was willing to play "second fiddle" for the sake of the kingdom of God. Mentoring relationships are not always predictable. Possibly the people we begin to mentor may even turn around and mentor us someday.

Paul and Timothy

What Paul learned from Barnabas, he invested into the life of Timothy and countless other young pastors. Yet Timothy was special to Paul. He probably led Timothy to the Lord during his first trip to Lystra (2 Tim. 1:2) and taught him the foundational principles of the gospel. Paul asked the younger man to accompany him on his second missionary journey, and from that point onward began to invest in him as his co-laborer in the gospel. Timothy shared in most of Paul's ministry—from Macedonia, to Achaia, to Ephesus, to Corinth, to Asia Minor, to Jerusalem, and even to Rome during Paul's first imprisonment. After Paul's release, Timothy again traveled with him, visiting various churches, but eventually Paul had him stay at the Ephesian church to take care of some problems. Their close relationship is verified by the fact that Paul names him as co-sender of six of his letters.

Paul's challenge to Timothy (2 Tim. 2:1-2) is a commission for all of us who will be in involved in mentoring relationships: "You then, my son, be strong in the grace that is in Christ Jesus. And the things you have heard me say in the presence of many witnesses entrust to reliable men who will also be qualified to teach others."

The pattern of mentoring, begun by godly men and women in biblical times, leaves us with valuable principles for mentoring relationships today.

Various Forms of Mentoring

As we have seen from Scripture, mentoring relationships may take various forms. Stanley and Clinton, in their book *Connecting: The Mentoring Relationships You Need to Succeed in Life*, identify seven types of mentoring relationships, moving along a continuum from the most intensive and deliberate to the least. Their main points can be outlined as follows.

Intensive

1. *Discipler*—Enablement in the basics of following Christ
2. *Spiritual Guide*—Accountability, direction, and insight for questions, commitments, and decisions affecting spirituality and maturity
3. *Coach*—Motivation, skills, and application needed to meet a task or challenge

Occasional

4. *Counselor*—Timely advice and correct perspectives on viewing self, others, circumstances, and ministry
5. *Teacher*—Knowledge and understanding of a particular subject
6. *Sponsor*—Career guidance and protection as leader moves within an organization

Passive

7. Model:

Contemporary—A living, personal model for life, ministry, or profession, who is not only an example but also inspires emulation

Historical—A past life that teaches dynamic principles and values for life, ministry, and/or profession

In this chapter we will concern ourselves only with the intensive and occasional mentoring relationships.

Under the intensive category of mentoring we have the discipler, spiritual guide, and coach. When most people think of mentoring, they usually envision this more intensive type of relationship, focusing on helping a person grow spiritually and utilize his or her spiritual gifts in ministry. It may be difficult, however, sometimes to separate mentoring relationships into three such categories. Often a relationship overlaps in all three areas or moves from one area to another as the relationship develops. I am a little uncomfortable with using the term *discipler*, as the authors do, since it is not used in this context in Scripture. Jesus Christ is the only person who makes disciples of Himself. We make disciples of Jesus Christ. By calling a mentor a discipler, we run the risk of usurping the authority that belongs only to Jesus Christ. It would be like calling someone a "Christianizer."

There certainly is a tremendous need for mentors who will help seekers and new Christians learn the basics of following Christ and then establish them in the fundamental disciplines of the Christian life. In the first few centuries of the early church, mentoring was a very structured process that all new converts went through. Yet lack of mentoring is one of the greatest weaknesses of the discipleship process in the church today. I believe that new believers need mentors who will get them grounded in the basic disciplines of the faith like prayer, Bible study, fellowship, and confession and stick with them until they are integrated into the nurturing body of the church. It is difficult to estimate how long this process might take. For each person it may be different. The most important thing is that the mentor sticks with the person until successful patterns of growth are established and the new believer has become interdependent with others within the larger church fellowship. This transfers the responsibility, over time, from the individual mentor to the collective body of Christ—the group that has been given the primary responsibility to "make disciples."

A mentor will often take the role of a spiritual guide to help a younger Christian deal with issues, questions, and concerns. The goal in this relationship should be for the mentor to guide the learner to Christ and His Word for answers. One danger, however, in such a relationship is for the guide to become like a "spiritual director" to the mentoree, fostering an unhealthy, long-term dependence on the mentor. While there may be a reason for a mentor to be very directive with a mentoree, the exercise of authority should not be done to gain control over the life of the mentoree, but rather to help the mentoree learn the value of submitting to the authority of Scripture.

Coaching is probably the form of mentoring used most. Usually it refers to the role of a mentor in helping another Christian learn a skill, task, or ministry. It could be teaching a person how to study the Bible, teach Sunday school, counsel troubled youth, or one of the many other tasks or ministries within the church. It could take the form of an apprentice relationship in which the mentor would work side by side with the mentoree, or it could look more like an occasional coach's huddle in which the mentor would periodically get together with a person to review strategies and failures. The intensity of the relationship and frequency of the interactions would depend on many factors.

Under the occasional forms of mentoring, Stanley and Clinton identify the roles of the mentor as a counselor, teacher, and sponsor. The role of the mentor as counselor serves to help the mentoree to deal with specific problems or issues in life. Such a relationship usually does not last more than a few sessions. Often a person might visit the mentor later on to deal with either a similar or different problem.

The role of a mentor as teacher is a one-on-one form of nonformal teaching that usually lasts for a given period of time until the mentoree has learned what was intended. Many times such mentoring relationships rise out of a more formal classroom situation in which a student wants more understanding or a deeper level of insight on a particular topic. In both of these mentoring situations involving either counseling or teaching, the mentoree usually initiates the relationship based on a significant problem or need. This point of contact becomes a "teachable moment" in a student's life that usually precipitates a learning experience the student will never forget.

The role of the mentor as sponsor is one in which the mentor introduces the new person in an organization or church to individuals, systems, and procedures that will help the new person become successful. The initial relationship between Barnabas and Paul was a sponsorship. In that relationship Barnabas integrated Paul into the life and ministry of the church. Although such a relationship could last a long time, it may only last until the new person is established in a network of relationships in the new situation. As you can readily observe, it would be ideal to match all new believers or church members with such mentors to assimilate them into the life of the church.

Mentoring relationships do not need to be long term to be significant. The key factor is the student's desire to learn, grow, or develop, and the mentor's willingness and ability to serve.

ESTABLISHING ACCOUNTABILITY STRUCTURES IN MENTORING

Over my years of mentoring different people in various ministry settings, from youth and pastoral ministries to college and seminary ministries, I have come to appreciate the need for structure in mentoring relationships. Yet whatever structure we develop to hold people accountable for their growth, we must keep it flexible and person-centered. Whatever accountability structures are used, they need to be developed cooperatively, with both parties having input. I have found that it is most effective if the mentorees take the responsibility for establishing "what" they want to learn and "how" they plan to learn it. The mentor then helps the mentoree to work out a more formal "contract" to document these learning goals and how they will be measured.

A format that has evolved from my practice over the years is based on God's challenge to His people in Deuteronomy 6:5: "Love the LORD your God with all your heart and with all your soul and with all your strength." The big idea from this text is that people need to love God with every aspect of their being. In more practical terms, it is helpful to divide the task of fulfilling this challenge into three major aspects:

1. Head/Knowing—intellectual growth
2. Heart/Feeling—emotional growth
3. Hands/Doing—growth in our skills, behavior, or practice

At the beginning of each new mentoring relationship, the mentoree is asked to set one to three goals in each of these areas and under each goal to identify one to three specific ways he or she will accomplish each goal. These goals and the action plan to accomplish the goals become the structure for the mentoring relationship. It keeps the mentoree focused on specific goals, and it reminds the mentoree of what must be done to learn those specific things. It provides both parties with an accountability structure. In their periodic meetings the two persons discuss the mentoree's progress toward the goals and deal with any issues or problems that have come up.

I have appreciated this format because it can be adapted to be more or less structured, depending on a person's need or temperament. Yet it holds the mentoree responsible to plan and design his or her own strategy for growth. As we mentioned earlier, when mentorees participate in the planning process, they are much more apt to see a plan through. This format has been very helpful in helping people to take responsibility for their own spiritual growth and development.

SUMMARY

Mentoring relationships are some of the most effective ways to help others grow and develop in their relationship with Jesus Christ. "As iron sharpens iron, so one man sharpens another" (Prov. 27:17). God has used such mentoring relationships to prepare some of the greatest leaders in the Bible. With the variety of different types of mentoring, people can plan and structure their relationship to meet a variety of needs. Intensive relationships may involve following up new believers, guiding someone in spiritual growth, or coaching someone to develop a particular ministry skill. Occasional relationships may involve counseling a person related to a specific problem he or she may be having, teaching a person one on one, or sponsoring people until they become a part of a church body or group. To be effective, mentoring relationships need to have some form of accountability so that both parties know what is expected of them. Yet it is important to keep the structure flexible according to the mentoree's needs and personality.

FOR FURTHER DISCUSSION

1. Why does there seem to be a greater need within our society for mentoring relationships?
2. What are some of the risks of mentoring someone?
3. Why might it be unwise to mentor someone of the opposite sex?
4. How would you feel if the person you mentored eventually took your place of ministry?
5. Why are accountability structures needed in a mentoring relationship?

III.

CONTINUING THE
GROWTH PROCESS

12

Being a Lifelong Learner

GROWTH IS A never-ending process for the Christian. This was true in the lives of such biblical personalities as Moses, David, Peter, and Paul, as well as almost every other person in the Scriptures that God used. The phrase, "Please be patient; God is not finished with me yet," expresses the sentiments of Christians today and in biblical times.

The apostle Paul emphatically stressed this point over and over. In Philippians 3:12-14, he talks of pressing on and straining for what is ahead. In 2 Timothy 4:7, he refers to the Christian life as a race and a continuing fight.

Adult educators often use the term "lifelong learning" when referring to the concept that learning continues in a person's life long after formal education stops. Although commencement speakers often remind graduates that the granting of their degrees does not indicate an end but a beginning, this idea seldom makes the impact the speaker desires. However, lifelong learning teaches this exact principle—the formal, school-oriented instruction children and youth receive is only the *beginning*, not the end, of learning. If our formal schooling has been successful, it will have provided us with the tools to continue learning for the rest of our lives.

Yet how do people make sure that they will continue to learn after they leave school? One of the keys is taking advantage of challenging learning opportunities that help adults integrate their life experience with their learning. Research indicates that adults prefer to learn using various learning styles, and they are often frustrated in the typical classroom setting, which tends to focus on only one learning style while ignoring others. A good mix of both formal and nonformal learning experiences provides a variety of ways of learning to challenge the adult learner.

FORMAL LEARNING

Formal Christian adult education is usually linked with structured classroom learning experiences. Following are some of the most common possibilities.

Adult Sunday School

In the context of the local church, Sunday school is an excellent opportunity for adult learning. Since adults have varying needs and interests, most churches provide elective classes on different topics and subjects. Often adults can choose from different teaching formats. Adults select the class that will be most valuable to them in their Christian lives and growth. At the same time, they determine personal goals for participating in the class, which may be slightly different from the goals of the course but will guide their own involvement in the class.

Evening Training Institutes

Individual churches or several churches in a community often cooperate to develop an adult training institute. These programs usually meet one night a week and often include course offerings in Bible, doctrine, and lay ministry topics. Some form of adult education credit leading to a certificate or diploma is often offered as well.

Colleges and Seminaries

As the older adult population continues to increase, Christian colleges and seminaries are providing more non-degree and degree programs geared especially for adults. Many schools offer courses at convenient times during the day, evening school classes, correspondence school courses, online courses, weekend classes, and summer school sessions, with fee structures more appropriate to part-time students. Online opportunities for Christian education are rapidly becoming a very popular way for nontraditional adult learners to continue their education. More and more school and ministry training sites are being added to the Web daily.

Adult Bible Studies

There are an increasing number of opportunities for growth in both large and small group adult Bible studies. Sometimes these study groups meet in homes, churches, community centers, or even businesses. Yet the goals are usually the same—to study and discuss God's Word in an informal setting, to apply biblical truths to daily lives, and to fellowship with one another. A growing variety of Bible study material is available to minister to almost any need. Studies are available for people from every walk of life and circumstance—women, men, couples, singles, new believers, the elderly, divorced, and even those trying to lose weight. Some studies focus on systematic or inductive Bible study, and others are more topical in their approach. Some are geared for evangelism while others help mature Christians grow in their faith. In order to grow, Christians need to be a part of a challenging Bible study group with other believers.

Seminars, Conferences, Workshops

Opportunities to be involved in seminars, conferences, and workshops for Christian adults have never been more available. Leadership and teacher training, marriage and family, and Bible content areas are popular topics at seminars and workshops. Many camps and conference centers provide a relaxed setting for adults to not only attend challenging lectures and seminars, but also to relax with family or friends. Denominational conferences also provide valuable opportunities for local churches and their members to learn and grow together. However, to achieve the full benefit of these meetings, specific personal goals must be determined prior to attending. It is a good idea after such retreats to discuss with family members or friends what to do with what is learned at such events. Plans should be formulated and recorded at the conclusion of the seminar, conference, or workshop for putting into practice what has been learned. Ideally, several individuals who attended the same conference could later meet to discuss personal reactions and applications.

Adult learning has both a personal and interactional component. Although each of these formal learning opportunities includes interaction with other adults, the full benefit of each learning experience will only be realized as individual adults determine personal learning goals prior to participating and make plans for application afterward.

NONFORMAL LEARNING

A phase of lifelong learning often overlooked is nonformal learning—the independent learning opportunities all adults participate in nearly every day. Whether it is seeking an answer to a problem through conversations, reading, or study, or a more structured independent learning project, we are constantly involved in nonformal learning. Following are some examples.

Personal Devotions/Bible Study

Whether it is reflecting using a daily devotional guide, studying a biblical or theological issue, or studying a book of the Bible, personal Bible study and reflection is one of the most significant learning experiences contributing to our spiritual growth. To help organize these learning experiences, it is a good practice to keep a notebook to record what we learn.

Sermons

Sermons can be excellent learning experiences if we take notes, discuss the main points with others, or critically reflect on the ideas presented. By studying the text ahead of time, a person can be better prepared to wrestle with the issues presented. Taking sermon notes in a Bible or a separate notebook helps a person to remember key points better and to refer to them at a significant time in the future. Some churches are turning their Sunday evening services into discussion groups focusing on the main points of the morning sermon. Such experiences help people to apply Scripture to their lives much more effectively.

Reading

Books, magazines, and journals covering every subject imaginable for Christians are available today. Regularly reading a journal or magazine of personal and spiritual interest can be a significant part of a growing believer's diet. It is also good to develop a habit of reading a book a month for challenge or encouragement.

Adult Learning Projects

Almost every day adults are involved in learning, whether it be researching an idea in a library or asking questions of an individual more knowledgeable in a particular area. People should determine what it is they desire to learn and then devise a course of action to achieve that learning goal. After setting up a learning plan, it is important to be accountable to some other person for accomplishing it.

ESTABLISHING LIFELONG LEARNING GOALS

Growing spiritually is a lifelong process that will only be complete when we see Christ face to face. We need to keep our eyes on that goal as we deal with the day-to-day struggles and frustrations. These are some areas that should be considered in establishing lifelong learning goals.

Head

As the believer's textbook for life, the Bible is the most important element in lifelong learning. An increased knowledge and understanding of the Scriptures should be a major goal of every adult believer. Those books of the Bible that are least known and understood should be studied more. At the beginning of each year, we should determine our personal goals for the study of the Scriptures and plan a learning strategy to meet those goals during the year. Theology, church history, Christian biographies, and Christian magazines should all be a part of the growing Christian's diet. Since all truth is God's truth, wherever it is found, we should also stay abreast of reading from stimulating secular authors.

Heart

We need to set goals in our life related to keeping our hearts and passions pure. Since the Bible teaches that growth in the Christian life comes from the inside out, we need to develop a growth plan that includes disciplining our inner life. Emotions such as anger, lust, hatred, bitterness, pride, resentment, and hurt, if left uncontrolled, can often destroy the life and ministry of a neglectful believer. Once again, to insure progress in these areas of our lives, it is imperative to have a close friend or mentor to hold us accountable. Since many of these issues have deep roots in our past, it may take time to deal with them. At some point it may even be necessary to see a professional counselor.

Hands

Each adult believer is gifted with abilities from the Holy Spirit for the edification of the church and fellow believers. These gifts and abilities, however, must be continually developed to bring glory to God. We must take advantage of every opportunity to grow in the area of our spiritual gifts, skills, and abilities. These opportunities may include instruction in teaching, leadership, mentoring, evangelism, counseling, visitation, or some other ministry skill. While discipleship in the church has tended to focus more on learning information about God and the Bible, Jesus emphasized not only knowing but also obeying what we know. We must make sure that we become not only good hearers of the Word but also good doers.

PUTTING IT ALL TOGETHER

Not every adult learning experience is beneficial. For adult learning to have an impact on our life, ministry, and spiritual growth, we must choose our learning experiences to suit our individual needs and goals. These principles may be helpful in organizing a beneficial individual learning plan that will help us to continue to grow and mature.

Determine Personal Goals

Any learning program requires specific goals and an action plan. These goals should be related to our needs in light of what God wants for our lives based on Scripture. A good place to begin is by examining our needs in each of the major areas of our lives—head, heart, and hands. In areas where the Holy Spirit reveals to us that we are weak, we set a specific goal that we will strive for, based on God's Word. In order to achieve a sense of balance in our growth, it is a good idea to pick at least one goal from each of the three areas.

Choose Learning Experiences to Meet our Goals

Next we should determine which formal and informal learning experiences will best achieve our goals. At this point people must evaluate their available time, learning preferences, opportunities, and other obligations. While a person may want to be involved in every learning opportunity available, it is necessary to be very selective about what we commit ourselves to. Often nonformal learning opportunities provide busy adult learners with the flexibility they need to achieve their goals. Matching our goals with the best learning experiences is the second step to achieving our goals.

How to Determine If Goals Have Been Met

To make sure that we accomplish our goals, we need to determine ahead of time how we will know if our goals have been met. Are there specific skills or attitudes that we want to learn? Are there areas in our life that we need to deal with? We need to identify specific areas of knowledge or behavior change that should be learned by the end of the learning experience. We need to clearly identify how we will know when the learning is complete and the goals have been met.

When our learning experiences work together to accomplish specific purposes, real growth and development will result. Creating and following through with an individual learning plan becomes a catalyst to our growth.

SUMMARY

Growth is a continual process for the Christian. Paul modeled his passion for continued growth by setting spiritual goals and continuously working toward accomplishing them. We should wisely follow his example.

Opportunities for lifelong learning abound for us today. Whether through formal or nonformal means, the believer needs to take advantage of every opportunity to learn, grow, and develop. By developing an individual learning plan, we will be more apt to take our learning seriously as we diligently strive to walk more closely with Christ and learn from Him and His Word.

FOR FURTHER DISCUSSION

1. Investigate the available formal learning opportunities that would be of interest to you. List those that could have potential for you in the next two years.
2. Investigate the available informal learning opportunities that would be of interest to you. List them as you did above.
3. Think of specific ways you could develop your ministry skills, increase your knowledge of the Bible, or deal with a personal struggle or habit. Develop an action plan related to each of these areas of learning or development.
4. Why is it important to have an organized plan for lifelong learning related to your spiritual life?
5. What ways do you learn best? What learning situations do you enjoy the most?

NOTES

CHAPTER 1
THE DYNAMICS OF SPIRITUAL GROWTH

1. Samuel M. Shoemaker, *How to Become a Christian* (Waco, Tex.: Word, 1953), 72.

CHAPTER 2
BECOMING A DISCIPLE OF JESUS CHRIST

1. W. E. Vine, *An Expository Dictionary of New Testament Words* (Old Tappan, N.J.: Revell, 1966), 316.

CHAPTER 3
THE CHURCH'S ROLE IN MAKING DISCIPLES

1. Gary C. Newton, "The Motivation of the Saints and the Interpersonal Competencies of Their Leaders," *Christian Education Journal*, Spring 1990, 9-15.

CHAPTER 7
FRUITFULNESS AND REACHING OTHERS FOR CHRIST

1. Robert E. Coleman, *Evangelism on the Cutting Edge* (Old Tappan, N.J.: Revell, 1986), 137.

BIBLIOGRAPHY

CHAPTER 1

Gangel, Kenneth O., and James C. Wilhoit, eds. *The Christian Educator's Handbook on Spiritual Formation*. Wheaton, Ill.: Victor, 1994.

Green, Michael. *New Testament Spirituality: True Discipleship and Spiritual Maturity*. Great Britain: Eagle Publishers, 1994.

Issler, Klaus, and Ronald Habermas. *How We Learn: A Christian Teacher's Guide to Educational Psychology*. Grand Rapids: Baker, 1994.

Lawrence, Brother. *The Practice of the Presence of God*. Old Tappan, N.J.: Spire, 1958.

LeFever, Marlene D. *Learning Styles*. Colorado Springs: David C. Cook, 1995.

Packer, J. I. *Knowing God*. Downers Grove, Ill.: InterVarsity Press, 1973.

Whitney, Donald S. *Spiritual Disciplines for the Christian Life*. Colorado Springs: NavPress, 1991.

Wilhoit, James C., and John M. Dettoni, eds. *Nurture That Is Christian*. Grand Rapids: Baker, 1995.

Tozer, A. W. *The Pursuit of God*. Camp Hill, Pa.: Christian Publications, 1982.

CHAPTER 2

Coleman, Robert E. *The Master Plan of Evangelism*. Old Tappan, N.J.: Revell, 1963.

Hull, Bill. *Jesus Christ Disciple Maker*. Grand Rapids: Revell, 1984.

Shoemaker, Samuel M. *How to Become a Christian*. Waco, Tex.: Word, 1953.

Wilkins, Michael J. *Following the Master*. Grand Rapids: Zondervan, 1992.

CHAPTER 3

Banks, Robert. *Paul's Idea of Community*. Grand Rapids: Eerdmans, 1980.

Hull, Bill. *The Disciple Making Church*. Tarrytown, N.Y.: Revell, 1990.

McIntosh, Gary, and Glen Martin. *Finding Them, Keeping Them*. Nashville: Broadman, 1992.

Spader, Dann, and Gary Mayes. *The Everyday Commission*. Wheaton, Ill.: Shaw, 1994.

Stevens, R. Paul. *Liberating the Laity*. Downers Grove, Ill.: InterVarsity, 1985.

Yancey, Philip. *Church: Why Bother?* Grand Rapids: Zondervan, 1998.

CHAPTER 4

Fee, Gordon D., and Douglas Stuart. *How to Read the Bible for All It's Worth*. Grand Rapids: Zondervan, 1982.

Finzel, Hans. *Observe, Interpret, Apply*. Wheaton, Ill.: Victor, 1994.

Sterrett, T. Norton. *How to Understand Your Bible*. Downers Grove, Ill.: InterVarsity, 1974.

Wald, Oletta. *The Joy of Discovery in Bible Study*. Minneapolis, Minn.: Augsburg, 1975.

CHAPTER 5

Baker, Howard. *Soul Keeping: Ancient Paths of Spiritual Direction*. Colorado Springs, Colo.: NavPress, 1998.

Foster, Richard J. *Prayer: Finding the Heart's True Home*. San Francisco: Harper, 1992.

Hybels, Bill. *Too Busy Not to Pray*. Downers Grove, Ill.: InterVarsity, 1998.

Jones, R. Wayne. *Using Spiritual Gifts*. Nashville: Broadman, 1985.

McRae, William. *The Dynamics of Spiritual Gifts*. Grand Rapids: Zondervan, 1983.

Murray, Andrew. *With Christ in the School of Prayer*. Old Tappan, N.J.: Revell, 1953.

Taylor, Howard and Florence S. *Hudson Taylor's Spiritual Secret*. Chicago: Moody Press, 1979.

Torrey, R. A. *The Power of Prayer*. Grand Rapids: Zondervan, 1924.

Willard, Dallas. *Hearing God: Developing a Conversational Relationship with God*. Downers Grove, Ill.: InterVarsity, 1999.

Winter, D., *Walking into Light*, a reinterpretation of the great devotional classic, *The Confessions of St. Augustine*. Wheaton, Ill.: Shaw, 1986.

CHAPTER 6

Bridges, Jerry. *The Pursuit of Holiness*. Colorado Springs: NavPress, 1978.

Crabb, Larry. *Inside Out*. Colorado Springs: NavPress, 1988.

Foster, Richard J. *Celebration of Discipline*. San Francisco: Harper & Row, 1978.

Hughes, R. Kent. *Disciplines of a Godly Man*. Wheaton, Ill.: Crossway, 1991.

Willard, Dallas. *Spirit of the Disciplines*. New York: HarperCollins, 1990.

CHAPTER 7

Aldrich, Joseph C. *Life-Style Evangelism*. Portland, Ore.: Multnomah, 1981.

Griffin, Emory A. *The Mind Changers*. Wheaton, Ill.: Tyndale, 1976.

Hybels, Bill, and Mark Mittelberg. *Becoming a Contagious Christian*. Grand Rapids: Zondervan, 1996.

Little, Paul E. *How to Give Away Your Faith*. Downers Grove, Ill.: InterVarsity, 1966.

Pippert, Rebecca Manley. *Out of the Salt Shaker and into the World*. Downers Grove, Ill.: InterVarsity, 1979.

Poe, Harry L. *The Gospel and Its Meaning: A Theology for Evangelism and Church Growth*. Grand Rapids: Zondervan, 1995.

CHAPTER 8

Bugbee, Bruce, Don Cousins, and Bill Hybels. *Network*. Grand Rapids: Zondervan, 1994.

Hohensee, Donald, and Allen Odell. *Your Spiritual Gifts*. Wheaton, Ill.: Victor, 1992.

CHAPTER 9

Carlson, Gregory C. *Understanding Teaching*. Wheaton, Ill.: Evangelical Training Association, 1998.

Hendricks, Howard G. *Teaching to Change Lives*. Portland, Ore.: Multnomah, 1987.

Pazmino, Robert W. *Basics of Teaching for Christians*. Grand Rapids: Baker, 1998.

Richards, Lawrence O., and Gary J. Bredfeldt. *Creative Bible Teaching*. Chicago: Moody Press, 1998.

Wilhoit, Jim, and Leland Ryken. *Effective Bible Teaching*. Grand Rapids: Baker, 1988.

Zuck, Roy B. *Teaching As Jesus Taught*. Grand Rapids: Baker, 1995.

CHAPTER 10

Clinton, J. Robert. *The Making of a Leader*. Colorado Springs: NavPress, 1988.

Dudley-Smith, Timothy. *John Stott: The Making of a Leader*. Downers Grove, Ill.: InterVarsity, 1999.

Gangel, Kenneth O. *Team Leadership in Christian Ministry*. Chicago: Moody Press, 1997.

Miller, Calvin. *The Empowered Leader*. Nashville: Broadman, 1995.

Reed, Bobbie, and John Westfall. *Building Strong People*. Grand Rapids: Baker, 1997.

Rinehart, Stacy. *Upside Down: The Paradox of Servant-leadership*. Colorado Springs: NavPress, 1998.

Steinbron, Melvin J. *The Lay Driven Church*. Ventura, Calif.: Regal, 1997.

Stevens, R. Paul, and Phil Collins. *The Equipping Pastor*. New York: The Alban Institute, 1993.

Warren, Rick. *The Purpose Driven Church*. Grand Rapids: Zondervan, 1995.

CHAPTER 11

Bruce, A. B. *The Training of the Twelve*. Grand Rapids: Kregel Publications, 1971.

Davis, Ron Lee. *Mentoring—The Strategy of the Master*. Nashville: Thomas Nelson, 1991.

Friedeman, Matt. *Accountability Connection*. Wheaton, Ill.: Victor, 1992.

Hendricks, Howard and William Hendricks. *As Iron Sharpens Iron*. Chicago: Moody Press, 1999.

Shea, Gordon F. *Mentoring—A Practical Guide*. Menlo Park, Calif.: Crisp, 1992.

Stanley, Paul D., and J. Robert Clinton. *Connecting*. Colorado Springs: NavPress, 1992.

CHAPTER 12

MacDonald, Gordon. *Ordering Your Private World*. Nashville: Thomas Nelson, 1985.

Peel, William Carr. *Discover Your Destiny: Finding the Courage to Follow Your Dreams*. Colorado Springs: NavPress, 1997.

Peterson, Eugene H. *A Long Obedience in the Same Direction*. Downers Grove, Ill.: InterVarsity, 1980.

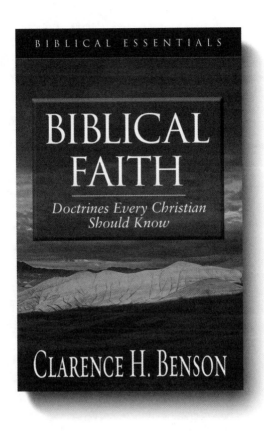

BIBLICAL FAITH:
DOCTRINES EVERY CHRISTIAN SHOULD KNOW
CLARENCE H. BENSON

Why do Christians study doctrine? You might say our faith depends on it. In a culture that promotes a variety of religions and argues that all are equally valid, it is essential that Christians know doctrine. Without sound doctrine, our faith is in danger of being distorted or destroyed. In *Biblical Faith,* Dr. Benson offers a concise, straightforward explanation of twelve basic doctrines. The book begins by discussing what evangelical Christians believe about Scripture and then explores doctrines from Creation and the Fall to heaven and hell. The most profound truths of the Bible are described in a way that is clear and easy to understand.

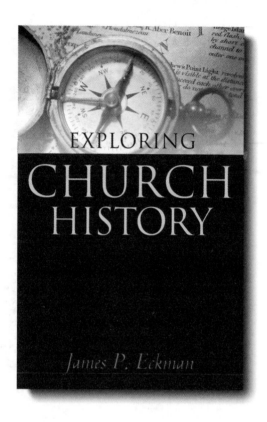

EXPLORING CHURCH HISTORY
JAMES P. ECKMAN

When we study church history, we are learning about more than just names and dates. We are exploring our own Christian heritage. And as we study the past, we also prepare ourselves for the future, because many contemporary issues are not new at all. A study of church history also gives an accurate understanding of the complexities and richness of Christianity. The church has suffered much, but a thorough look at its past reinforces our conviction that the church will triumph. Dr. James Eckman leads readers through church history from the Pentecost to the present. This basic introduction, done chronologically, emphasizes the theological process and developing consensus within the church on what the Scriptures teach, as well as the institutional development of the church.

EXPLORING THE OLD TESTAMENT
SAMUEL J. SCHULTZ AND GARY V. SMITH

It is imperative for every growing Christian to study all of the Bible. In *Exploring the Old Testament*, Samuel Schultz and Gary Smith survey the content of the Old Testament so that readers will understand each book's events and themes. Chapters conclude with projects, questions, and exploration activities that not only test readers' grasp of the materials but also provide opportunity for more detailed and intensive study. This book acquaints people with the Old Testament's major divisions and its amazing unity as a whole. Both authors are well-equipped to guide readers through the Old Testament. Schultz is Professor Emeritus of Bible and Theology at Wheaton Graduate School, and Smith is Professor of Old Testament at Midwestern Baptist Theological Seminary.

EXPLORING THE NEW TESTAMENT
WALTER M. DUNNETT

Exploring the New Testament takes a survey approach that will deepen your knowledge of God and enrich your understanding of the Bible. Readers will gain an overview of the entire New Testament, consider the respective writers and their work, and understand the purpose, outline, main content, and leading features of each New Testament book. All of these elements lay a solid foundation for understanding the message and revelation of Jesus Christ. The chapters end with application activities and discussion questions. Author Walter Dunnett served on the faculty of Northwestern College.

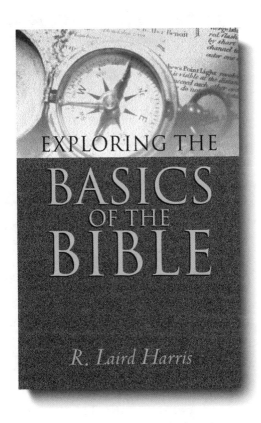

EXPLORING THE BASICS OF THE BIBLE
R. LAIRD HARRIS

The Scriptures are God's Word to us. We should personally read them, study them, meditate upon them, and most of all, practice them. But the first step to a truly enriching study of the Bible is understanding the basics behind its writing. R. Laird Harris's introductory book explores important questions that many wonder about: Who wrote the Bible? How was it written? Why should I believe that it is God's Word? What about its seeming contradictions and problems? All these topics and more are covered in this thorough treatment of the truth about the Bible. The book concludes with chapters on study helps and Bible study methods, as well as a list of resources for enrichment. Harris is widely known and respected for his biblical scholarship, as well as his past teaching and leadership at Covenant Theological Seminary.

BIBLICAL ESSENTIALS

EVIDENCE AND TRUTH

Foundations for Christian Truth

ROBERT J. MORGAN

EVIDENCE AND TRUTH: FOUNDATIONS FOR CHRISTIAN TRUTH
ROBERT J. MORGAN

How do we know that Christianity is true? How do we respond to doubters who say that our faith is only about fictional stories and unfounded feelings? In *Evidence and Truth*, Robert Morgan takes readers step-by-step through the well-documented historical and physical evidence that supports the claims of Christianity. He deals with such topics as the resurrection of Christ, the complexity of creation, the reliability of the Bible, and the changed lives of believers. Whether the reader is looking for personal answers or wants to be prepared to answer a friend, this book will help. *Evidence and Truth* offers a solid intellectual basis from which the reader can take a step of faith and experience the ultimate assurance that comes from God's Spirit. A graduate of Columbia International University and Wheaton College Graduate School, Morgan pastored for nearly twenty-five years and has authored several books.

Since 1930

Evangelical Training Association

THE MINISTRIES OF EVANGELICAL TRAINING ASSOCIATION

(ETA)

Experienced – Founded in 1930.
Doctrinally Dependable – Conservative and evangelical theology.
Educationally Sound – Engaging all adult learning styles.
Thoroughly Field-Tested – Used by a global constituency.
Recommended – Officially endorsed by denominations and schools.
Ministry Driven – Committed to quality training resources for equipping lay volunteers to serve Christ more effectively in the church.
Affordable – Attractive and reasonably priced.

For many local ministries, the most important step to an effective lay leadership training program is locating and implementing an inspiring, motivational system of instruction. ETA curriculum is available as traditional classroom courses, audio and video seminars, audio and video CD-ROM packages, and other resources for your classroom teaching or personal study.

Contact ETA today for free information and a 20-minute video presentation. Request Information Packet: Crossway Partner.

EVANGELICAL TRAINING ASSOCIATION
110 Bridge Street • PO Box 327 • Wheaton, IL 60189
800-369-8291 • FAX 630-668-8437 • www.etaworld.org